Teaching Children to Read in Diverse Communities:
A Practical Guide
for Reading Success

SECOND EDITION

Teaching Children to Read in Diverse Communities: A Practical Guide for Reading Success

Timothy R. Blair

University of Central Florida

Academic Media Solutions

Affordable - Quality Textbooks, Study Aids, & Custom Publishing

Teaching Children to Read in Diverse Communities: A Practical Guide for Reading Success,
2nd Edition, Timothy R. Blair

Paperback ISBN: 978-0-9823241-9-6
Online ISBN: 978-0-9890496-3-4

Copyright © 2013, 2008 by Timothy R. Blair.

ISBN-10: 0-9823241-9-7
ISBN-13: 978-0-9823241-9-6

Printed in the United States of America by Academic Media Solutions.

Dedication

*To Jeanné, my sweetheart and wife of over 45 years;
my sons, Tim and Bill; my daughters-in-law, Donna and Tara;
and my four wonderful grandchildren, Andrew, Christian,
Wyatt, and Carson*

Preface xi

PART 1 DIVERSITY AND READING
INSTRUCTION 1

**1 *Embracing Our Differences: What Teaching
Reading Is All About* 3**
Today's Classrooms 4
Diversity 4
Poverty 6
Importance of Reading 9
Effective Reading Programs in Diverse Settings 9
Teacher Effort 13
Overview: Fundamentals of Reading Instruction 14
 The Reading Process 14
 Stages of Reading Development 14
  Emergent Literacy 15
  Formal Reading 15
  Wide Reading 15
  Independent Reading 15
 The Complete Reading Program 16
Personal Observations: Teachers-in-Preparation 16

**2 *Finding Out about Your Students: Culture,
Attitudes, and Emotional and Instructional
Needs* 19**
Assessment Process 20
"Reading" Students 20
Student Background Experiences and Culture 21
Student Self-Perceptions and Needs 22
Emotional Maturity 24
Instructional Needs 25
Priority Decision-Making 26
Continuous Assessment and Reflection 28
Model of Assessment-Instruction 28
Personal Observations: Teachers-in-Preparation 28

3 *Providing Differentiated Reading Instruction* 31
Differentiated Instruction 32
Grouping Students 32
Teaching Reading 33
 Pre-Planning Considerations 33
  Importance of Being a Self-Monitor 33
 Essential Instructional Components in the Reading
  Period 34
  1. Readiness, Review, and Motivation 34
  2. Vocabulary Development 35
  3. Thinking Activity 35
  4. Skill/Strategy Development 35
  5. Fluency Development 35
  6. Coaching for Understanding While Reading 35
  7. Guided Reading and Story Retelling 35
  *8. Read Aloud and Independent Reading and/or Writing
   Activities 35*
  9. Practice and Reinforcement 36
  10. Review 36
  11. Evaluation and Reflection 36
 Teacher Behaviors in Effective Reading Programs in
  Diverse Communities 36
 The Necessity of Practice 40
Personal Observations: Students 41

4 *Parents and Reading* 43
Parental Influence on Children 44
Realities in Diverse Communities 44
Help for Parents and Classroom Teachers 46
Culturally Sensitive Strategies for Fostering Parental
 Involvement 49
Parental Expectations 52
Personal Observations: Parents 52

PART II CRITICAL TEACHING PERFORMANCE AREAS: CAPSULE SUMMARIES   55

5   *Communicating High Teacher Expectations*   57
What It Is and What Research Can Tell Us   58
Teacher Behaviors   58
Teaching Strategies   58

6   *Emphasizing Oral Language Development*   61
What It Is and What Research Can Tell Us   62
Teacher Behaviors   62
Teaching Strategies   63

7   *Developing Prior Knowledge*   65
What It Is and What Research Can Tell Us   66
Teacher Behaviors   66
Teaching Strategies   66

8   *Teaching Phonemic Awareness*   69
What It Is and What Research Can Tell Us   70
Teacher Behaviors   70
Teaching Strategies   70
Activities   71

9   *Teaching Vocabulary*   73
What It Is and What Research Can Tell Us   74
Teacher Behaviors   74
Teaching Strategies   75
Activities   76

10   *Teaching Phonics and Word Recognition*   79
What It Is and What Research Can Tell Us   80
Teacher Behaviors   81
Teaching Strategies   81
Activities   82

11   *Developing Fluency*   85
What It Is and What Research Can Tell Us   86
Teacher Behaviors   86
Teaching Strategies   86

12   *Fostering Comprehension*   89
What It Is and What Research Can Tell Us   90
Teacher Behaviors   91
Teaching Strategies   91
Activities   92

13   *Developing Critical Thinking*   95
What It Is and What Research Can Tell Us   96
Teacher Behaviors   96
Teaching Strategies   96

14   *Teaching a Story: Guided Reading*   99
What It Is and What Research Can Tell Us   100
Teacher Behaviors   100
Teaching Strategies   100

15   *Developing Understanding in Content Reading*   103
What It Is and What Research Can Tell Us   104
Teacher Behaviors   104
Teaching Strategies   104

16   *Common Core State Standards Based Reading Instruction*   109
What It Is and What Research Can Tell Us   110
Teacher Behaviors   111
Teaching Tools and Strategies   112
Close Reading Lesson Planning Model Exemplar 113

17   *Technology for the Reading Program*   115
What It Is and What Research Can Tell Us   116
Teacher Behaviors   117
Teaching Tools and Activities 117
    Assistive Technology (AT) 117
    Blogs 118
    Classroom Wikis 118
    Digital Texts and Digital Libraries 118
    Digital Storytelling, Writing, and Presentation Applications 119
    Animation/Avatars 119
    Create a Video/Movie 119
    Writing/Storyboard 119
    Glogster (http://edu.glogster.com/) 120
    Graphic Organizer and Mind Map Software 120
    Tablets and Mobile Applications 120
    Twitter (https://twitter.com/) 120
    Wordle 121

18 *Promoting Independent Reading* **123**

What It Is and What Research Can Tell Us   124

Teacher Behaviors   124

Teaching Strategies   125

  Book Week Celebration Each Fall Season   125

    Introduction   125

    Activities Prior to Book Week   125

    Activities during Book Week   126

  Classroom Ideas to Promote Recreational Reading
and Writing   127

Appendix A   Capsule Review of Reading Skills and Strategies   129

Appendix B   Explicit/Direct Instruction   133

Appendix C   Graded Paragraph Inventory (GPI)   135

Appendix D   Parent Guide: Helping Your Child Become a Better Reader   163

References   R-1

Index   I-1

Preface

Teaching Children to Read in Diverse Communities: A Practical Guide to Reading Success, Second Edition, continues to cover the essential research-based balanced reading strategies for the elementary and middle grades and current topics in the teaching of reading in a succinct and clear framework. School systems across the country are continuing their focus on differentiated instruction and flexible grouping to implement a balanced literacy/reading approach with increased emphasis on the instructional levels of students. As in the first edition, this practical and concise coverage continues to be presented along with attention to the realities of increased student diversity and the growing number of children living under the poverty line in our classrooms today.

The federal government's National Assessment of Educational Progress (NAEP), popularly known as the Nation's Report Card, has documented for many years the lower reading achievement of students of diverse backgrounds in the United States. Children who are unable to read sufficiently are at a high risk for dropping out of school. Children who do learn to read well are able to break the cycle of poverty and become productive individuals. The primary goals of this book are to help teachers teach children to read in our nation's schools and to develop in teachers a positive mind-set or set of dispositions to be successful with all children, especially children from homes low in literacy, ethnic minority children, and children who have limited proficiency in English.

This new edition reflects two significant trends in the teaching of reading in our elementary schools—trends affecting the primary functions of the teacher of reading. First, with the focus on high-stakes testing and research-based materials, an entire new chapter on the new Common Core State Standards (CCSS) has been added. Learning in our schools will be accelerated through the merging of state standards with the new Common Core standards. Most school districts have embraced these new standards, and classroom teachers must use their reading materials to address the standards with their children. These new standards will add increased rigor to the curriculum as students will be required to read more difficult material in all courses, including a wider mix of literature and nonfiction. Students will need to locate information, draw inferences, make conclusions, and compare and contrast. The new Common Core State Standards will alter what children will learn, how they learn it, and how we measure learning.

Second, with the trend of increasing technological developments and their effect on the teaching-learning process, an entire new chapter on technology has been added to help teachers understand how best to use new tools to enhance both their teaching and their children's learning (that is, leveraging technology to engage the digital generation!). All teachers are in the process of making the transition from traditional instructional design practices in their teaching to interactive student methodologies using a variety of mobile devices. The hottest instructional products for the classroom today are Web-connected multipurpose devices, such as tablets and mobile phones.

Part I, Diversity and Reading Instruction, begins with discussion of the growing diversity found in today's schools, poverty and its effects on schooling, and the program components of effective reading programs that beat the odds and are successful serving diverse communities. Chapter 2 presents a discussion of the importance of assessment in the learning process, highlighting a youngster's culture, self-perception, needs, emotional maturity, and performance or instructional level and specific skill needs. Appendix C contains a complete assessment tool (the Graded Paragraph Inventory) for determining a student's instructional level. Chapter 3 highlights the importance of providing differentiated instruction in the classroom. Readers are presented with the essential instructional components in the reading period and with effective teacher behaviors that guide the teaching of reading in diverse classrooms. Chapter 4 centers on the important role that parents play in the learning process. Culturally sensitive strategies are provided for teachers and practical suggestions for parents are provided so they can be an integral part of their child's reading improvement. In addition, Appendix D contains a parent guide to utilize in designing and delivering a parent education course or program centering on helping parents teach their children to read in the home.

Part II, Critical Teaching Performance Areas: Capsule Summaries covers the major components in the teaching of reading. Chapters 5 through 18 deal with (in sequential order) teacher expectations, oral language development, prior knowledge, phonemic awareness, vocabulary, phonics, fluency, comprehension, critical thinking, guided reading, content reading, Common Core State Standards (CCSS) based reading instruction, technology for the classroom, and independent/recreational reading. For each chapter, concise and to-the-point sections include: what it is and what research can tell us, effective teacher behaviors to implement the topic at hand, and a discussion of practical, research-based teaching strategies to implement in the classroom.

This book emanates from a unique collaborative initiative "Reading Camp Program," which is a partnership between a College of Education and a Department of Families, Parks, and Recreation in a large metropolitan city. This unique program prepares both undergraduate education majors and graduate masters in reading students, not in a public school setting, but at two inner-city community neighborhood centers. During the Fall and Spring semesters, this collaborative program takes place on Saturday mornings with undergraduate teacher education students and daily during the summer term with graduate reading masters students.

The Reading Camp Program is currently in its fourteenth year of operation. The two community centers are located in a poor, yet historic African-American neighborhood in a large city where residents are succeeding against a myriad of social and economic challenges. University students receive instruction in culturally responsive reading methods, tutor low-income children from kindergarten to grade seven, and then participate in debriefing sessions to reflect on their teaching and prepare for the next tutoring session. The undergraduate and graduate students participating in this experience continue to try out and refine the many research-based teaching techniques explained in the text.

In addition, while the children are being tutored in reading at the community centers, a "Parent Education Program" is provided for their parents, teaching them specific teaching techniques to help their children improve in their reading abilities in the home. Appendix D contains the Parent Guide "Helping Your Child Become a Better Reader." This guide is utilized for the parent program with specific instruction, teaching strategies, and suggestions for parents to teach their children to read in the home.

The aim of this text is to help teachers learn not only up-to-date scientifically based reading strategies but also learn to value and act upon a student's culture, family, community, language, interest, and past experiences in the classroom. The authentic responses sprinkled throughout various points in the margins of the text are actual responses from the teacher education students teaching reading in the Reading Camp Program at the community centers, the children being tutored, and their parents. These responses are intended to give further meaning and personal insights to various aspects of teaching children in diverse communities to read.

It is the sincere wish of the author that readers utilize the information presented in this book to become increasingly cognizant of what they are doing or not doing, what needs to be improved, what needs to be modified or expanded or omitted, what factors impede teaching reading, and how students react to what the teacher is doing. Our children in our diverse communities deserve knowledgeable and thinking teachers of reading who are constantly striving to provide them with an appropriate education.

I wish to extend my thanks and appreciation to the hundreds of children tutored in the Reading Camp Program, to the numerous undergraduate and graduate university students who participated as reading teachers, to Mrs. Dana Dodd Vaughan, Reading Camp Coordinator at the Dr. J.B. Callahan Neighborhood Center and the John H. Jackson Community Center, and to the parents who made certain their children attended the Reading Camp Program and also participated in the Parent Education Program, for their invaluable participation and contributions. I am grateful to my many undergraduate and graduate students, classroom teachers, and reading coaches for their reactions to several parts of the book. I wish to thank Sarah Adams Morton of the Stanley Switlik Elementary School in Marathon, Florida, and Lourdes H. Smith of the University of Central Florida for their valuable contributions to the book.

Finally, sincere appreciation is extended to Daniel Luciano, President and Founder of Academic Media Solutions, for his expert guidance and vision and to my production manager, Victoria Putman, for her expertise in the preparation of this book.

Diversity
and Reading
Instruction

Embracing Our Differences:
What Teaching Reading Is All About

Today's Classrooms

Teaching reading in our schools is a rewarding and exciting experience. Today, as in years past, teaching reading is also a major challenge and a complex process. Our classrooms have always been diverse, but now they are changing at a more rapid pace than ever before. Students represent countless racial, cultural, and ethnic backgrounds, and an increasing number of children are poor. The major premises of this book are twofold: The first is the firm belief that all children in our diverse communities can become skillful and motivated readers, and the second is that you, the teacher, have a significant impact on whether or not children in your class are successful in learning to read. Regardless of your students' background, what you teach, how you teach, and how you treat students will have lasting effects on every student in the classroom.

Children in our classrooms today truly exemplify the fact that we live in a diverse society. Capitalizing on and embracing this diversity are what make teaching in today's schools so enjoyable and at times painful. Even though we share many more similarities than differences, children are wonderfully different. Teaching children to read requires you to realize this fact and to embrace the wide range of differences and needs found in classrooms. Teachers of reading must recognize that capitalizing on differences is an indispensable aspect of their profession. Recognizing differences, accepting them, embracing and celebrating them, and then planning sound reading instruction based on this knowledge is what separates teachers who attempt to meet individual needs from those who do not. If all reading instruction could be the same for all children in each grade, teaching reading would be easy and relatively boring.

While children from all backgrounds can experience difficulties in learning to read, it is widely documented that low reading achievement is highest among poor children, ethnic minority children, and children who speak languages other than English at home (Donahue et al., 1999; Anderson, 1994). The common characteristic linking all of these groups is poverty, not the color of their skin. Rosenshine (2002), noted researcher on teacher effectiveness, reviewed the research literature on teaching students from low-income homes and concludes:

> Since 1963, a great deal of time, money, and effort has been devoted to closing the gap in reading scores and bringing children who are on free and reduced lunch (FRL) to grade level on standardized tests at Grade 3 and above. To date, we have not been very successful. There have only been a few schools with 70% or more of FRL students and where students are reading at grade level, at the end of third grade, on a standardized test. (p. 273)

Diversity

Our public schools in America reflect two continuing and growing realities: the diversity of students and the increasing number of poor children. We live in the most diverse country in the world. Not surprisingly, diversity has always been a reality in our schools and in the teaching of reading. Students are different in a multitude of ways—cultural history, race, social awareness, emotional maturity, psychological well-being, cognitive abilities, physical maturity, thinking abilities, creativity, preferred learning style, learning rate, language facility, socioeconomic level, and personal interests, to name a few. Speaking of the rich diversity in human characteristics, Brown and Kysilka (2002) state:

The wide variety found in even a small handful of students offers exciting possibilities to the teacher who knows how to take advantage of these differences. In multicultural and global education, the diversity of humans is seen as a richness to be enjoyed, treasured, and protected. Teachers and students must not see diversity as a problem. The challenge is not the diversity itself but tapping into the diversity in a positive way. (pp. 16–17)

In today's schools, many students speak a dialect other than Standard English, and many are learning English as a second language (ESL). There are many dialects in the United States, and each dialect is logical and governed by a set of internal rules. As teachers, you must show respect for a nonstandard dialect, while at the same time modeling Standard English. Furthermore, a student's competence is unrelated to his or her use of dialect. Dialectal errors made in reading may or may not interfere with a student's progress. It is important not to penalize students for dialectal errors in reading as long as comprehension is unaffected.

A large percentage of students have a native language other than English. It is not uncommon to have students whose native language is Spanish, Haitian-Creole, Polish, Navajo, or Vietnamese, to name just a few in your classroom. The census of 2000 shows that nearly one-fifth of school-age children in the United States speak a language other than English at home. Hispanic students constitute a majority of non-English speakers in U.S. schools. Recent U.S. Census Bureau reports indicate that one of every seven people in the United States is Hispanic, and this number is rising due to immigration and birthrates. The population growth for Asians is second in the United States and is growing as well for the same reasons. Additionally, most immigrants to the United States are young and in their 20s and thus at the age when people have children.

Many students whose native language is not English may experience difficulties learning to read in English. Many of these students have not had an abundance of oral language experiences in English in the home, do not understand spoken English, and know little written English. Sound reading instruction in both the student's native language and English is recommended. In addition to detailing language competencies for ESL students, the *ESL Standards for Pre-K–12 Students* (1997) exposes three myths with regard to second language learning:

Myth 1: ESL students learn English easily and quickly simply by being exposed to and surrounded by native English speakers.

Myth 2: When ESL learners are able to converse comfortably in English, they have developed proficiency in the language.

Myth 3: In earlier times, immigrant children learned English rapidly and assimilated into American life. (p. 3)

More cultures are represented in our classrooms today because the United States is continuing to become more culturally diverse. Driving the growing diversity is the continuous flow of immigrants. One very important reality in teaching today is that *you will teach students with cultural backgrounds different from your own*. This one fact is what makes teaching so intrinsically satisfying and at the same time so complex. As a member of the teaching profession, you have the responsibility to value and embrace students from diverse linguistic, racial, cultural, ethnic, religious, and economic backgrounds.

Cultural differences influence student performance and should influence classroom instruction (Brooks, 2006). For example, students' understanding of text will be better if they are reading and interacting with materials that are familiar to their culture and background experiences. Bottom line, it's important to pay attention to culture. Accepting this realization and making adjustments in your instruction is the hallmark of an effective teacher in diverse communities. Au (1993) labels this type of teaching as "culturally responsive instruction" and defines it as being "consistent with the values of students' own cultures and aimed at improving academic learning" (p. 13). Thus, classroom teachers need to adjust or differentiate their reading instruction to meet the natural strengths of the cultures represented in their classrooms. Diller (1999) emphasizes the importance of knowing a student's culture and its relationship to providing sound instruction:

> We must realize that culture is a viable teaching tool. We must seek first to get to know each child as an individual, including understanding the child's background. If the culture is unfamiliar, we must find help through children's literature, colleagues who know about that culture, and the children and parents themselves. Essentially, we find a guide into the culture. (p. 827)

Poverty

In addition to diversity, the second reality facing teachers and our schools is the increasing number of children living in poverty in the United States. Poverty exists in all areas—rural, suburban, and urban—and occurs in all races. Harold Hodgkinson (1999), a noted demographer, labels poverty as the "universal handicap," with social class more important than race.

Twenty-one percent of all children under the age of 18 in the United States live in poverty, and this percentage increases to 43% for African American children and to 41% for Hispanic children (*Youth Indicators 1996*, 1996). Fifty-three percent of children raised by single mothers live in poverty. Sixty-three percent of African American children and 68% of Hispanic children of single-mother households live in poverty in the United States. Hewson and Kahle (2003) report that large urban districts educate 35% of all students living in poverty, 30% of all English language learners, and nearly 50% of minority children. A recent study of the Washington-based Tax Policy Center (Burman & Wheaton, 2005) found that more than 25% of American children (consisting of 19.5 million children, of whom nearly 50% are African American and 46% are Hispanic) belong to families that are too poor to fully qualify for the $1,000-a-year child-tax credit.

Sadly, inequalities in the quality of our public schools are all too evident just by driving by schools in poor neighborhoods and schools in affluent neighborhoods. It is not only differences in the physical buildings and facilities themselves; the quality of the curriculum and of the human and material resources available to children in poor districts in many instances is not equal to that available to their more-affluent counterparts. The quality of life in many of our schools is not in keeping with our American ideals. In Jonathan Kozol's book *Savage Inequalities: Children in America's Schools* (1991), he chooses the correct word—"savage"—in the title to characterize the inequalities in our public schools.

Poverty is a vicious condition that can, among other things, rob children of the numerous opportunities to learn that are afforded to their more-affluent peers. The variable "opportunity to learn" is perhaps the most powerful variable in education. Many low-income children are not given the opportunity to experience the wide range of background experiences, crucial opportunities, and type and quality of interactions with language and books that will foster achievement in our schools, and this relates specifically to reading development. Thus, many low-income children are more likely to be at a disadvantage in terms of "reading" opportunities than other children.

Poverty directly affects student achievement. Without a doubt, there is an achievement gap between poor and affluent children (Closing the Achievement Gap Section, 2004. Furthermore, this gap is established even before children begin school. Denton and West (2002) of the National Center for Education Statistics (NCES) conducted a national study of children entering kindergarten and found that poor children, on average, are significantly behind other children in the areas of health, social skills, and academic achievement. Furthermore, poor children, unlike their more-affluent counterparts, actually fall back in achievement and lose ground during the summer months (Allington & McGill-Franzen, 2003). It is of particular interest that in relation to school achievement, the strongest effects of poverty are felt when poverty is viewed as a collective unit, such as a school or neighborhood, rather than as an indicator of the low-income status of an individual child. Snow, Burns, & Griffin (1998) provide the following summary of research on socioeconomic level (i.e., SES) and reading achievement:

> We are not saying here that SES is not an important risk marker. What we are saying is that its effects are strongest when it is used to indicate the status of a school or a community or a district, not the status of individuals. A low-status child in a generally moderate or upper status school or community is far less at risk than that same child in a whole school or community of low-status students. (p. 127)

Lyon (2001) agrees, and in his statement to the Subcommittee on Education Reform of the Committee on Education and the Workforce in the U.S. House of Representatives, he comments:

> Unfortunately, reading failure is disproportionately prevalent among children living in poverty. Specifically, in 1998, 64% of African American and 60% of Hispanic students in the U.S. (two groups that experience disproportionate rates of poverty) read below the basic level. Indeed, in many urban districts the percentage of students in the fourth grade who cannot read at basic level approaches 70%. (pp. 3–4)

Thus, this achievement gap is also between racial and ethnic minority and majority students, as well as poor and affluent students. Yet, it must be emphasized that difficulties affecting school performance are present among all children—urban, suburban, or rural—regardless of whether they are rich or poor. Still, the realities children of poverty must face each day are many and complex. We can no longer ignore poverty and its effects not only on U.S. society as a whole but especially on the children. Political, economic, educational, health, and social realities, and corresponding pressures, are realized and heightened for children in low-income areas of the United States.

The problems associated with being poor and living in a poor neighborhood that affect school performance and this achievement gap include:

- Many low-income children are part of families who lead very stressful lives.

- Many parents work two or three jobs at minimum wage to try and satisfy the needs of their families, leaving little extra time for helping their children with schoolwork.

- Many parents lack information concerning community institutions.

- Many of the children's neighborhoods are still segregated from positive health and educational opportunities that other children readily access.

- Many low-income children are exposed to a "different print environment" than their more-affluent counterparts; that is, low-income neighborhoods are many times characterized by having fewer libraries and bookstores, and in the home, there is less exposure to computers, the Internet, interactive videos, books, daily newspapers, and magazines. Implications for teachers regarding these differences in print environment among children include considerably less opportunity for these children to be aware of the concept of a word, print awareness, individual phonemes in words, letter and sound recognition, and word learning (all critical qualities of successful beginning readers).

- Children may get too little sleep, and poor nutrition may be present.

- Many times, children's health, educational, social, and emotional needs do not receive adequate attention because basic survival needs are a priority.

- For many children living in poverty, there is no tomorrow (time occurs only now, not in the future), little goal-setting (i.e., deferring pleasure for a future goal), and only survival in the present.

- The children's neighborhoods often have disproportionate percentages of crime, drug abuse, unemployment, reported child/neglect cases, juvenile arrests, and homeless shelters. Home ownership rates and median household income are low.

- Many of the children's parents face economic insecurity that forces them to make impossible choices daily (for example, should I stay at home to take care of my sick child and miss a day's pay, or leave my child at home alone? Should I pay the car loan this month or put dinner on the table? Should I pay for utilities or food? Should I pay the rent or mortgage or food? Should I pay for health costs or food?).

- Many children and their parents face language and immigration barriers each day that makes successful living complex.

- Many children live in housing projects where tight living quarters increase stress and the likelihood for violence. School is a safe place for many children because they receive healthy meals and spend the day in a heated environment during the winter months.

- Tight living conditions in the home oftentimes are disorganized, and this quality spills over into the classroom environment.

- Many children have poor self-esteem and unmet emotional needs. Often, unmet emotional needs are tied to undesirable behavior in school, as children attempt to satisfy their unmet emotional needs in the classroom rather than attend to the curriculum at hand.

- Many times, parents (and their parents) did not have positive experiences in school, and this attitude is passed on to the children. Because of this one reality, some children may be indifferent to school and actually resist your efforts to teach them.

- Many parents don't know how to help their children in school or to be advocates for them.

- Many children come to school with many difficulties that they do not wish to share with their teachers. Of course, there are exceptions: Many first-grade teachers will attest to the fact that first-graders will tell their teachers much of the happenings in the home.

- Many poor children begin kindergarten behind in formal oral language development and possess limited vocabularies, factors that are directly related to future success in reading. These children often did not have quality preschool experiences and were not given the opportunity to play with language (i.e., they spent little time talking with adults, singing songs, playing word and language games, and having books read to them orally). Thus, many children had different experiences with language that did not prepare them for success in our present school curriculum.

Most importantly, however, even though many children and their parents must overcome tremendously distracting hurdles on a daily basis, *low-income parents do value literacy, and low-income children can and do learn to read at high levels, given quality instruction that is responsive to their needs. Poor children are surprisingly resilient, want to learn, and are just as smart as affluent children!*

Importance of Reading

Children who experience success in learning to read not only are successful throughout their school experience but also in life. The ability to read enables children to open up a whole new world of imagination, wonder, information, and excitement. Successful students use reading as a tool to satisfy a variety of purposes, ranging from reading for specific information to satisfy a job requirement to reading fine literary works for pure enjoyment. These students learn the "how" of reading and develop the desire to read and learn on their own. Low-income children who struggle in learning to read often fail in school and are more likely to drop out of school than other children. These children also are at greater risk of experiencing various social and economic concerns, including continuing in the poverty cycle, low-paying jobs, and crime. Yet, despite these realities, many low-income students become literate and lead successful, productive lives. This is because these students received high-quality reading instruction.

Effective Reading Programs in Diverse Settings

It is unacceptable that a large number of low-income and minority children fail to learn to read. Stressing how poverty is such a powerful predictor of reading performance, Pearson (1997) boldly states, "The irony is that we seem best able to help those students who need our help the least." All children can and do become successful readers when they participate in a high-quality reading program. The key term in this statement is *high quality.* Unfortunately, there is a history of major differences in the educational experiences afforded to low-income children versus their more-affluent peers. After reviewing numerous studies on the subject, Hiebert (1996) observes:

> …we can conclude that access to high-quality reading instruction is not guaranteed for all children. This statement is most true for those students who depend on schools for that access: the children of low-income families. (p. 15)

Richard Allington has reported on these differences for a number of years (Allington, 1977, 1983, 2006; Allington & McGill-Franzen, 1989). Speaking directly to the instructional differences, Allington and Walmsley (1995) state:

> Low-achieving readers are more likely to be asked to read aloud rather than silently, to have their attention focused on word recognition rather than comprehension, to spend more time working alone on low-level work sheets than on reading authentic texts, and to experience more fragmentation in their instructional activities. Instructional tasks then differentiate the experiences of children who have little difficulty acquiring reading and writing abilities and those who have some or much difficulty. Much of the difference in reading strategy between high- and low-achievement readers can be explained by the differences in the instructional tasks emphasized. (p. 29)

Reading programs in diverse settings that beat the odds and are successful have the following seven emphases:

1. *A balanced and differentiated program of reading instruction based on an assessment of student strengths and weaknesses is provided.* "Balanced reading instruction" combines both teacher-directed explanation and modeling of essential reading skills and strategies and student-directed independent reading activities. "Differentiated reading instruction" is adapted or modified to suit a student's current performance level and specific skill needs in reading, taking into account his or her emotional, personal, and cultural needs.

   Your reading instruction must have a blend of both explicit/direct instruction and independent learning activities, and must take into account each student's interests, needs, and culture. The focus here is on matching exactly your instruction to what students need in terms of the five components of the reading process—phonemic awareness, phonics, fluency, vocabulary, and comprehension (National Institute of Child Health and Human Development, 2000)—as well as students' emotional, personal, and cultural needs. Each of the five components of the reading process is fostered through instruction and an abundance of practice in meaningful text. This includes both placing students in reading materials at an appropriate level of difficulty and teaching them exactly what they need to advance their reading abilities.

2. *Teachers and administrators model the elements of the teacher effectiveness literature, especially the procedures related to opportunity to learn, explicit/direct instruction, and academic engaged time.* "Opportunity to learn" refers to teaching the content that students are expected to know and providing sufficient practice for students to learn the content. "Explicit/direct instruction" is instruction in which the teacher directly explains, demonstrates, or models new learnings to students, followed by sufficient guided and independent practice to ensure student mastery. "Academic engaged time" is time in which students are actively working on the objective of the lesson at hand, sometimes called time-on-task or on-task behavior.

   These three elements of teacher effectiveness are implemented with an emphasis on small-group instruction, specific goal setting, daily monitoring of student progress, and a highly interactive, collaborative style of classroom learning. It is essential that important reading objectives are "covered" (i.e., taught and practiced) and that a high amount of student time-on-task or engagement is maintained to ensure student mastery and learning. Of particular note is the recommendation to teach the specific components of phonemic awareness, phonics, fluency, vocabulary, and comprehension through the explicit/direct model of instruction (National Institute of Child Health and Human Development, 2000). This instructional model lends itself to nurturing the other two elements: opportunity to learn and academic engaged time. Teachers who use this teaching model for specific learning objectives consistently produce higher-than-average achievement in their classes (Rosenshine & Stevens, 1995). Appendix B presents an expanded explanation of this approach. At the heart of this teaching approach is the direct explanation, modeling, or demonstration of a given skill or strategy by the teacher. In some classrooms, this ingredient is notably absent, with little explicit/direct instruction on how to read. Delpit (1991) presents an illustrative example of this condition in recounting an experience of observing a child in a literature-based reading program:

> In California, I saw a black child who was in a class where the kids were supposed to read a piece of literature and then respond to it. The child clearly couldn't read the selection. When asked about the situation, the teachers said, "Oh, he can't read it, but he'll get it in the discussion." Perhaps it's good that he will be able to get it in the discussion, but at the same time nobody is spending time teaching him what he also needs to learn—how to read for himself. (p. 545)

3. *Students' culture, language, and background experiences are accepted and celebrated in teaching reading.* Culture affects how children learn in the classroom. Teachers of reading who recognize this fact take advantage of their students' family and culture, including their language, background knowledge, and experiences, in designing effective learning experiences (Edwards, 2004). Many times, diverse students have extensive background knowledge and experiences in areas different from their suburban counterparts. Successful teachers of diverse students pay attention to and learn from what their students say and encourage students to ask questions and give their opinions.

4. *The focus in the reading program is on students' strength—what they already know, their comprehension of ideas—while at the same time, teaching word identification or decoding skills.* Being sensitive to and learning about students' culture, community, and background knowledge will help in making educational decisions. Teaching must be based (you have no other choice!) on what students already know. Next, the teaching of reading is concerned with two broad categories: word identification and comprehension. Both areas are interrelated and interdependent. Yet, for purposes of placing students in appropriate reading materials for instruction, it is especially important to favor the comprehension ability over word identification accuracy in determining the appropriate level at which the students need to receive instruction. The primary reason is that many students of diverse backgrounds speak a different dialect and/or are learning English as a second language. It must be remembered that language itself is culturally grounded, and as such, diverse students may be at a disadvantage in communicating effectively in the language used in schools. Students' word identification skills and formal oral language abilities will probably be weaker than their comprehension abilities. Thus, if word identification is given equal weight, many students will be placed at a much lower instructional level. Placing students in reading materials based on their

comprehension abilities, while at the same time providing explicit, concentrated instruction on their word identification weaknesses, is recommended.

5. ***Both instruction and extensive authentic practice are planned for in the area of oral language development in standard or mainstreamed dialect.*** Many students from diverse backgrounds come to school behind in language development without having extensive modeling and practice in the oral language used in our schools. Comparing three-year-olds in both high socioeconomic status (SES) families and low SES families, Hart and Risley (1995) found that the children in high SES families had vocabularies as much as five times greater than low SES children. Because reading ability is closely linked to oral reading facility, it is recommended that students receive concentrated instruction and practice in oral language development, including planned interactive talk experiences.

6. ***A cognitively challenging curriculum, including instruction on critical thinking abilities, is designed and implemented.*** Many reading programs in low-achieving schools emphasize word identification over comprehension instruction, and the comprehension instruction frequently centers on literal or factual comprehension. Critical comprehension or the teaching of thinking strategies is often given little time in the curriculum (Haberman, 1996, 2005). All students need opportunities to think at higher levels to become strategic readers and truly literate.

7. ***Teachers and administrators take personal responsibility for delivering a high-quality instructional program, spending time getting to know every student personally, emphasizing positive behavior, and communicating high teacher expectations, knowing that this will pay off with more student effort and more positive attitudes toward learning.*** Expectations are so powerful that we still don't know all the facets of this trait. Many students do not come from environments where they are told they are bright and can succeed. Successful reading programs are characterized by having teachers and administrators who are totally committed to every child, assume that all children will be successful, realize it is their responsibility to carry out a high-quality program, and in effect say, "These children will learn and be successful—no excuses." In addition, successful teachers and administrators continually hold and communicate high expectations to students and continually expect and communicate to their students that they will put forth a high degree of effort in their classroom activities. Illustrating these points is the following observation by Bonnie Flanagan (1997), a new fourth-grade teacher in a poor urban Chicago elementary school:

> As a white teacher in an African American school, I needed to gain the acceptance of the students, parents, and other teachers. . . . The children are accustomed to a learning environment that focuses on discipline. . . . I put more emphasis on goal-setting and tend to set high expectations for my students. (p. 1)

The preceding seven program emphases require much time, effort, and knowledge on the part of the teacher and the entire school administrative team. It is almost certainly easier to stick with the easy method and be satisfied with the minimal results obtained with minimal effort. *However, successful teachers and administrators take the time and expend the effort necessary in these seven areas, not because they like to work hard, but because they seek satisfying results from their labors.*

Teacher Effort

We know that success in reading depends on the type and quality of instruction. In this sense, teachers need to expend "effort" in specific areas to make a difference in children's learning. However, not all of the hard work and efforts are helpful. Sometimes, hard work and extra efforts serve other purposes: They act as "window dressing"—cosmetic but not really very effective. Since teachers can expend their time and efforts in a variety of ways in teaching reading, it is important that you recognize which efforts are more helpful in teaching, since clearly, not all of them are. Successful teachers work hard and expend a great deal of effort in the seven areas discussed in the previous section (and specific areas and techniques are summarized in Part II of this text). Teachers who exert more effort in these seven areas in teaching reading in diverse classrooms likely will produce significantly higher reading achievement scores in their classes than teachers who exert a lesser amount of effort. The key here is teacher effort—knowing where to put your time and effort in teaching reading.

The concept of "teacher effort" is helpful in explaining, in part, the difference in student achievement scores across teachers. Blair (1975) found that teachers who exerted more effort in selected areas in teaching reading produced significantly higher reading achievement scores in their classes than did teachers who exerted a lesser amount of effort. Teachers were rated on an instrument evaluating efforts to: (1) secure and utilize a variety of materials, (2) provide differentiated instruction, (3) keep records of student progress, and (4) arrange conferences dealing with an individual student's progress. Results indicated that classes taught by high-effort teachers were associated with higher gains on the achievement measure for primary and intermediate grades. The finding that teacher effort makes a difference at both primary and intermediate grade levels is important in that it implies that hard work in teaching makes a difference at any grade level.

Many reasons or causes for reading difficulties in children are "negative" in nature, such as physical or psychological problems or family background realities, and you have little control over these. However, educational reasons or causes for reading failure over which you have complete control include, for example, your assessment program, the reading strategy you choose to teach, and the particular reading approach you emphasize with your students.

These causes for possible reading failure that *are under the influence of the teacher* are "optimistic" causes. Raths (1975a) introduced this concept of an "optimistic criterion," meaning one that teachers can do something about immediately in the classroom, unlike IQ, which cannot be manipulated by professionals. In speaking about the selection of variables for educational research, Raths states:

> As the explanation advanced in a hypothesis suggests optimistic variables, ones that can be manipulated through policy decisions or through re-training, the importance of research is enhanced beyond measure. (p. 6)

The seven components mentioned in the previous section embody optimistic causes. It is on these optimistic causes that you must develop the disposition to focus your efforts in teaching children to read. The specific instructional areas and teaching procedures are detailed in Part II of the text.

Through research over the past 40 years, both on the reading process and the teaching of reading, we know how to advance children's reading abilities. Teaching is a decision-making process, and where teachers focus their efforts in the teaching of reading is the real key to the success or failure of their program. Samuels (2002), a member of the National Reading Panel, addresses this topic directly when he states:

> The review of the research literature which we did uncovered definite procedures that teachers ought to be using in the classroom if they want to guarantee that virtually all kids will be able to read if they put the effort into it.

You have control over your instructional practices and classroom climate. Knowing where to place your efforts in teaching children makes the difference. With this power, teachers directly affect the achievement of children in their classrooms. *You are the key to the success or failure of a youngster learning to read. Where you focus your efforts in teaching will have lasting effects on your children.*

Overview: Foundations of Reading Instruction

The past 30 years have produced significant research on the reading process and on the components of effective classroom reading instruction. The following is a summary of these important understandings and areas in the teaching of reading.

The Reading Process

Reading is the communication of ideas through writing. We use written language to express ideas. Each reader must identify and interpret these written symbols based on his or her prior knowledge, and make sense of the author's intended meaning. Thus, reading is an active process of constructing meaning from written text in relation to the experiences and knowledge of the reader. In this view, the reader relates or makes connections between the new information in the text to existing or prior knowledge (what the reader already knows). Reading is also viewed as an interactive process in which reading comprehension is the result of many factors interacting while the reader processes text. From this perspective, reading is the fusion of various factors of the text itself, the context or environment in which reading occurs, and factors associated with the reader. Also, reading is an active communication process in which the reader uses effective strategies to comprehend text. At one time or another, one set of factors (e.g., text) may influence comprehension more than another (e.g., context and reader). In a sense, communication occurs between the author and reader, with the reader ultimately arriving at the text's meaning based on his or her own prior knowledge and experience. To fully achieve this communication and understanding, the effective teaching of reading requires a focus on the areas of phonemic awareness, phonics, fluency, vocabulary, and comprehension (National Institute of Child Health and Human Development, 2000).

Stages of Reading Development

It is important that teachers of reading realize that learning to read is meaning related and is a developmental process in which learners in their own way proceed to become mature readers. Children progress through four broad phases of reading: (1) emergent literacy, (2) formal reading, (3) wide reading, and (4) independent reading.

Although these phases are discussed separately here, no sharp lines of demarcation separate them. In addition, learning to read is an individual activity, and each child's reading abilities evolve in a unique way. Still, it is helpful in planning instruction to know the different phases through which most children proceed in acquiring one of the most crucial skills of their lives—reading.

Emergent Literacy

Parents and early childhood programs play vital roles in the earliest phase of the development of a child's reading ability. Learning to read begins at birth, long before formal schooling, and parents are their children's first teachers. This phase is more than just reading readiness. The term *emergent literacy* encompasses interactions in reading and writing from birth to age five or six. Parents can help ensure their child's success in reading by sharing good books and fostering a positive attitude toward reading. Both actions informally teach and reinforce a variety of essential readiness skills and abilities, including oral language development, listening ability, phonemic awareness, letter recognition, print awareness, word awareness, and learning of individual words. Likewise, various preschools and television programs such as *Sesame Street* have similar goals involving the development of proper attitudes and oral and written language abilities.

Formal Reading

Beginning in kindergarten (and in some preschools as well), children usually begin more formal development of their reading abilities through a commercially developed program such as a basal reader, a language arts or language experience program, or a combination of these. Both independent word identification and comprehension abilities are systematically taught and reinforced during this phase. Reading is continually encouraged as leisure-time activity, with text comprehension as the ultimate goal. Toward the end of this phase, readers spend less time on word identification and can concentrate more on comprehension. Readers in this phase are made aware of story structure and are guided to use their background of experiences to anticipate and interpret meaning.

Wide Reading

The wide-reading phase usually corresponds with grades four through six and marks a dramatic shift from reading and learning simple narrative and expository text to more complex narrative and expository text—for example, math, science, and social studies books. Successful reading in these areas demands not only general reading abilities but also specific reading-study skills needed for each content area, knowledge of various expository text structures, and ability to seek out, organize, and evaluate new information from a variety of sources. Mastery of basic skills in reading does not predict the ability to read materials with a particular content for specific purposes. Children need to be taught the skills and strategies necessary to pursue the ever-increasing knowledge in all fields—that is, they must learn how to learn.

Independent Reading

The final phase of reading development is characterized by readers who read a lot, enjoy reading, read different types of text differently depending on their purpose, monitor their own comprehension, and make adjustments while reading to comprehend satisfactorily. In this phase, readers are adept at interpreting both narrative and expository text to fulfill their purpose. In essence, they are able to think critically about, and know how to use, what they read.

The Complete Reading Program

For reading development to proceed in a meaningful fashion, classroom time needs to be balanced with respect to goals, characteristics of students, and the quality of students' reading experience. Although each classroom and grade level will differ because of learner goals and characteristics, an effective reading program spans four areas of learning—*instructional, content, recreational,* and *corrective*—as shown in Table 1-1.

Every grade needs to include experiences in each area; however, time should not be split equally among them. More word-identification instruction and practice and less content instruction are required in the primary grades (1–3). In the intermediate grades (4–6), little time is spent on word identification (except advanced word study), and more time is devoted to fluency, vocabulary, and content reading and studying strategies. In every grade, comprehension-related instruction should be the primary focus.

Personal Observations: Teachers-in-Preparation

How was it beneficial working with students from diverse populations in learning to teach reading?

"I was able to work with an English Language Learner (ELL) student and really was able to implement many of the recommended strategies I learned about in my university class."

"It allowed me to interact with students of different backgrounds than my own. I learned to be sensitive to students' family and cultural backgrounds."

"Each child's own culture is so important—I never realized this until I actually tried to motivate urban students to read a story."

Table 1–1 Components of a Complete Reading Program

Components	Learning Experience	Materials
Instructional	Focused and sequential learning experience in word identification and comprehension strategies	Literature books, basal readers, language experience, teacher-made materials
Content	Focused and sequential learning experience in content reading and study strategies	Content texts, content materials, newspapers, magazines, teacher-made materials
Recreational	Wide independent reading, promoting reading as a leisure-time activity	Library books, magazines, book clubs
Corrective	Focused instruction and practice on weak skills and strategies	Literature books, supplemental materials, computer programs, teacher-made materials

"I learned so much from my students—I heard all the statistics and numbers about low-income students, but now I truly know the academic and emotional struggles many students must face every day."

"My first few lessons were too easy for my children. They looked at me like, 'Are you serious?' I found out that urban students want to be challenged and can learn whatever I expect from them."

"I found that the students struggled over background knowledge I assumed they knew. I had not anticipated or planned for this and had to adjust my teaching. It takes a lot of effort to make learning enjoyable for both the teacher and students."

"I was so unsure of myself and my teaching abilities on the first day. I came away from this experience with confidence in my abilities and so much knowledge about living in an urban area."

"I now realize teachers must be concerned with all children—especially those not as fortunate in our society."

"I realized many of my children were so tired from staying up late at night and were hungry, and learning to read was not the top priority I thought it would be in their lives."

"I learned to capitalize on my students' interests in teaching reading."

Finding Out about Your Students:
Culture, Attitudes, and Emotional and Instructional Needs

Assessment Process

At the heart of effective teaching is the teacher's ability to assess and diagnose students' needs. Students learn more from teachers who are skilled in assessment than teachers who are not knowledgeable in this area. Any time a reading teacher plans learning experiences for an individual student or a group of students, the experiences are based on an assessment or diagnosis. An effective reading teacher must be a skilled diagnostician in both affective (i.e., cultural influences, attitudes, self-perceptions, interests, and emotional needs of students) and cognitive (i.e., a student's instructional level, vocabulary abilities, content knowledge, and knowledge of specific reading skills and strategies, to name a few) areas.

"Reading" Students

A cliché among educators today is "The teacher is the single most significant factor in determining whether students will be successful in learning to read." This statement implies a knowledgeable, skillful, exciting, and caring teacher. We have all had teachers like that, who enjoyed what they were doing and instilled a love for learning in their students. These teachers put life into the subjects they taught and cared deeply about their students as human beings. Such teachers were concerned with not only the cognitive growth of their students but also with how their students felt about themselves, their abilities to be successful, and their culture and background experiences. The key to being such a teacher with all students, especially diverse students, is your ability to know both their affective and cognitive needs and translate this information into a meaningful reading program. James Raths (1975b) coined the term *reading students* to embody this key concept, which is a process of being sensitive to and inferring students' motivations, interests, and needs through an accumulation of a variety of information. Raths hypothesizes that some teachers are "better readers" of students than others and that this ability pays off in student learning. In a sense, "better readers" are able to put themselves in their students' shoes, empathize with their feelings and needs, and translate these insights and information into an instructional program for students. Some of the indicators of "reading" students include the following:

- Be sensitive to signs of frustration and lack of confidence.

- Notice those classroom situations where a student is successful, motivated, and self-confident.

- Be sensitive to students' reactions, preferences, and involvement in different group settings.

- Know students' present instructional levels and specific skill needs.

- Be aware of students' backgrounds, families, and culture.

- Know students' attitudes, interests, hobbies, likes, and dislikes.

- Notice students' ability, or lack of ability, to think on a critical level.

- Notice any differences in student understanding of narrative text versus expository text (i.e., content books).

- Be sensitive to and take note of students' learning rates and preferred learning styles.

- Translate your observations and knowledge into instructional changes during the school day.

Student Background Experiences and Culture

Successful teaching begins with fulfilling student needs. One way to assess your students' needs is through informal conversations that reveal interests, experiences, family, cultural heritage, and attitudes. The informal interest inventory presented in Figure 2-1 lists questions designed to learn this information from your students. To make learning to read alive and exciting, teachers must strive to get to know their students and to make their instruction relevant to students' interests and backgrounds. The most successful teachers can "read" their students and determine strong areas of prior knowledge, interests, and needs. In addition, information gleaned from these questions will point you to books and other printed materials that match students' interests and motivation. Talking with students about their prior experiences, family, and culture will help you plan meaningful discussions about books. Also, information from the informal discussions often will help guide the psychological teaching approach you select to use with students.

Another way to develop sensitivity to your students' culture and background is to informally interview your principal, supervisors, other teachers, parents, social workers, and community center personnel about your students' backgrounds and culture. You can also surf the Internet to learn about the dominant characteristics, interests, dialects, values, beliefs, and family and community traditions of your students.

Knowing about the culture of your students also has a direct relationship to teacher expectations and subsequent student achievement. It is common knowledge that a teacher's beliefs can have positive or negative effects on how well students learn. In all classrooms, and particularly those in diverse settings, teachers need to be aware of their students' cultures, the importance of expectations, and how expectations are communicated into actions.

Another increasingly available means to learn about your children's cultures is to take a university course on a specific country or area of the world. Illustrative of this approach is the report by Zequeira (2006) on a university project aimed at reducing cultural barriers toward immigrant Haitians. The reporter describes the experience of Amanda Cobb, an Orlando, Florida, reading teacher, who had a reluctant reader. The student was Haitian. In describing the student's reticence to read, Cobb states, "Initially, I thought it was a shy thing. . . . But it was more like 'My accent is weird and I don't want people to say anything about me.' It surprised me." Cobb proceeded to teach reading to this student, and the student's reading abilities improved. To avoid future misunderstandings and a delay in delivering effective instruction, Cobb enrolled in a new course at the University of Central Florida designed to teach teachers about the Haitian culture and how to make instructional materials culturally appropriate. The U.S. Census Bureau reported in 2004 that 57,000 Caribbean immigrants from English- and French-speaking nations were living in Metro Orlando, with Haitians comprising the largest group. The university course helps teachers learn about the country of Haiti, its history, and the culture of its people. Reflecting on completing the course and thinking ahead to next year's teaching, Cobb states, "I've got poems I'm thinking about using

Figure 2-1 Informal Interest Inventory

- Do you have brothers and sisters? If so, how old are they? Tell me about them.

- Tell me about your parents and grandparents.

- Has your family always lived in this city?

- What holidays are most important in your family?

- Can you read or write in another language? If so, which language?

- Do your parents speak another language other than English? What is it?

- What do you usually do on the weekends?

- Do you have any hobbies? If so, tell me about them.

- Do you like sports? Which ones? Do you play sports at the community center or in a city league? Tell me about it.

- What is your favorite sport to watch? Do you follow the team statistics and highlights in the newspaper or on the computer?

- Do you have a pet? Tell me about your pet.

- What is your favorite movie?

- What are your favorite TV programs?

- Do you like computers? Do you have a computer at home? What programs do you run on your computer?

- Do you like music? What kind of music do you like?

- What places have you visited?

- If you could go anywhere in the world, where would you go?

- What kinds of things do you like to do during the reading period?

- What is one thing you don't like about your school?

and an article written by Christopher Columbus on Haiti. . . . But what I think I'm going to be saying in Creole a lot is: 'Do your work.'"

Student Self-Perceptions and Needs

Regardless of the grade level you are teaching or observing, it does not take long to notice the positive and negative consequences of student self-perceptions on success in school. Student self-perceptions and feelings are clearly linked to student learning. They can help or hinder achievement. Students who have healthy self-perceptions about themselves are not afraid to learn something new and are motivated to learn new reading strategies and content. However, students who have developed negative self-perceptions are less confident and frequently will not participate fully in new learning experiences in school. Many times, these students perceive the learning of new reading strategies and content as another opportunity to fail. By taking the following steps, classroom teachers show a concern for student self-perceptions and their importance in learning to read:

- Capitalize on students' interests and backgrounds in planning instruction.

- Monitor students' feelings, involvement, and success in reading activities and provide timely feedback.

- Design instructional activities in which all students have a reasonable chance of success.

- Communicate personal interest and friendliness to each student, stressing that he or she will be successful in the classroom this year.

Another powerful factor affecting the learning process is the fulfillment of personal needs. According to this concept, a student will perform in the classroom according to his or her perceived fulfillment of needs. Since students have different needs, teachers must learn to recognize these needs and experiment with numerous options when interacting with students. Ausubel and Robinson (1969) addressed this point over 35 years ago:

> Since teachers are constantly exhorted to attend to the child's needs, interests, and abilities, it is no doubt useful for teachers to be acquainted with these general need systems. If a hierarchy concept has any validity, such knowledge is important because a child in the classroom may be attempting to satisfy some prepotent need when the teacher is attempting to activate the desire to know and understand. (p. 355)

Abraham Maslow (1954) proposed a theory of motivation based on human needs. He viewed human needs in a bottom-to-top hierarchy and believed they were interrelated and interdependent to one another. He theorized that an individual focused on one need until that need was satisfied before moving on to the next need. His hierarchy or ladder of needs had five levels: physiological, safety, love and belonging, self-esteem, and self-actualization. Academic abilities or needs occur in the self-actualization stage; however, if lower-order needs are largely unmet, it is unlikely that much academic progress can be achieved.

In this view, one of the best ways to meet students' needs is to offer a sound instructional program based on student needs. There is no substitute or commercial material to replace good teaching, which provides the bridge between basic student needs and instructional needs. Combs (1982) stresses the importance of meeting personal needs in the learning process. However, he goes on to place student needs in a wider perspective:

> That good teaching begins with helping students fulfill basic needs does not mean good teaching stops there. . . . It is not enough to simply satisfy student needs. The genius of good teaching lies in helping students discover needs they never knew they had. The most effective schools and teachers do more than satisfy existing student needs; they turn students on. They help students perceive ever-broader horizons and greater depths of experience. (p. 29)

Another important realization for teachers of diverse children to bear in mind is students' search and need for "meaning." James Macdonald (1964), noted curriculum theorist, described two growth experiences of "personal meanings" and "culturally defined meanings." Personal meanings are those family experiences, cultural traditions, background knowledge, and self-concept that students bring to the learning situation.

These experiences are tied directly to life experiences and culture, and are unique to each individual. Culturally defined meanings are those understandings that the school system and teachers decide students need to learn. While it is important for teachers to introduce students to a large array of broad, culturally defined meanings, teachers must also be sensitive to the broad range of personal meanings brought to the classroom. As emphasized earlier, it is important to build on what students already know in teaching new content and understandings. As teachers, you have to integrate the two types of meanings in teaching children and realize that students will always filter new learnings through their own self-concept and family background.

Emotional Maturity

Students' emotional needs play an important role in the learning process. Louis Raths (1972) hypothesized that students have eight emotional needs: (1) belonging, (2) achievement, (3) economic security, (4) love and affection, (5) sharing and respect, (6) freedom from fear, (7) freedom from intense feelings of guilt, and (8) the need for self-concept and understanding. If a student's emotional needs are met, he or she feels good and approaches new activities with confidence. Raths hypothesized that *unmet* emotional needs lead to negative self-esteem and reluctance on the student's part in approaching new classroom learning situations.

Students who are emotionally mature handle new situations, periods of frustration, and stress with appropriate reactions. At such times, a teacher might say that a certain student is motivated and giving great effort to an activity. It is certainly desirous to have students who cannot wait to get started on an activity and who perform beyond minimum expectations. On the other hand, students who are not emotionally secure may respond to a given situation with aggression, hostility, withdrawal, or other compensating behavior. Such behaviors are considered symptoms of emotional needs. Since a student's emotional behavior influences learning, it is crucial for teachers to be aware of these emotional needs and to create a classroom environment that promotes each student's emotional growth.

Because each student has different needs, it is imperative that individual differences be recognized and treated accordingly. For example, one student may thrive in an activity that is beyond his or her level, but that same activity may devastate another student of similar ability. Likewise, a student may have a great emotional need to be a member of a group. If the teacher utilizes various grouping plans to involve this student continually with his or her classmates, greater learning and emotional growth can be attained.

Your daily interactions with your students and the classroom environment you create are the keys to promoting their emotional maturity. Your sensitivity toward students will directly affect their emotional growth as well as their cognitive growth. Being able to respond appropriately to them depends on how well you know them and how sensitive you are to their needs—in other words, your ability to "read" your students.

Being sensitive to the emotional needs of students creates a climate of acceptance and trust in which learning can flourish. James Raths (1969) lists a number of practical guidelines to foster students' emotional security in the classroom including:

- The teacher's behavior must be highly consistent.

- Children need to know the limits of acceptable behavior.

- Students want a teacher who can save them from extremes of humiliation.

- Students feel more secure when the teacher is relaxed and pleasant.

- Students feel more secure when the teacher's explanations, directions, and comments are clear and to the point.

- Students feel more secure when they are with a teacher whom they consider to be fair.

- Students feel more emotionally secure when they are respected.

- Students feel more secure when school becomes a place they can "live," not a place where they must serve time. (pp. 73–75)

Instructional Needs

Effective reading teachers at any grade level select and modify instructional goals in relation to what their students need; therefore, the decisions teachers make need to be based on assessment information gathered on their students. Effective teachers collect relevant information on students, interpret and synthesize this information, and plan and prescribe instruction according to student needs.

The crucial first step in assessment is to determine the student's instructional level. This helps you match the difficulty level of stories and materials to be used for instruction with a particular student. The probability for success in reading is raised if a student is working on the "just-right" level—that is, at their instructional level. Working at one's frustration level (i.e., when the book is too difficult) all but eliminates the chance of producing significant achievement in reading.

Once the student's instructional level has been determined, other important areas of reading development needing attention are revealed. However, it must be acknowledged that our assessment instruments are not totally precise, and a student's instructional level is affected by many factors, such as interest and background experiences. Thus, any determination of instructional level must always be accompanied by continuous assessment and subsequent adjustment.

The three functional reading levels of students, including the instructional level, are:

- The instructional or "just-right" level, at which the student can complete material with some support from the teacher (challenging but not too difficult). This is the teaching level.

- The independent or "easy" level is the highest level at which the student can complete material with no support from the teacher (especially important for assigning homework and books to be read independently).

- The frustration or "too-difficult" level is the lowest level at which the student cannot handle the material, and of course, this level should be avoided for instruction.

An effective method to determine these functional levels is to administer an informal reading inventory (IRI). There are many excellent commercially published informal reading inventories. Appendix C contains an IRI, the *Graded Paragraph Inventory (GPI)*. Administration of the GPI requires students to read paragraphs of increasing difficulty to determine the highest level at which they can read with satisfactory comprehension. A more-detailed explanation of this test and its administration is contained in Appendix C, but the basic steps of its administration are as follows:

1. Drop back two grade levels from the student's present grade placement, and use that corresponding paragraph as the starting point.

2. Discuss the topic of the passage and review background knowledge with the student.

3. Pronounce the names of the proper nouns in the passage.

4. Ask the student to read the passage aloud.

5. As the student is reading, complete a running record or record the number of oral reading errors made on the examiner's sheet. The five errors or miscues to note are (a) words not known, (b) words mispronounced, (c) words substituted for a word in the paragraph, (d) words omitted, and (e) words inserted.

6. After the student finishes reading the passage orally, remove the passage, and ask the student to tell you about the paragraph (i.e., to retell what happened in the paragraph). Ask the student questions starting with *who, what, where, when, why,* and *how* to ascertain the student's comprehension of the passage.

7. If, in your judgment, the student has comprehended at least 70 percent of the passage, continue on to the next passage.

8. Repeat steps 2–7 until the student fails in comprehension. Even if a student fails the criterion for word identification, it is recommended you continue the test until comprehension is unacceptable. When this point is reached, the test is over.

9. The last level for which the student passes the comprehension criteria is the instructional level, the next higher level is the frustration level, and the level just prior to the instructional level is the independent (or easy) level. For example, if the student's instructional level was determined to be three, the frustration level would be four and the independent level would be two.

Priority Decision-Making

After determining the instructional level, you know the level of books and materials you will need to use for your instruction. Now you must initially decide on specific areas needing attention to advance your student's reading abilities. It is important to remember that learning to read is being ready for one step after another. A parallel can be drawn to the construction of a house. The foundation of a house must be poured before the frame is started. The same concept holds true for reading skills and strategies.

Analyzing the types of errors or miscues the student made in orally reading the passages and in comprehending the passages will give you initial areas to target for instruction. In addition, you can administer other informal or formal tests to determine specific student strengths and weaknesses. Table 2-1 is a guide to your priority decision-making, indicating other important areas probably needing instruction and continuous assessment, depending on the student's instructional level.

Table 2-1 Priority Decision-Making

Student Instructional Level	Probable Areas for Instruction
Preprimer, Primer, and 1	• Sight words • Oral language development • Print and word awareness • Comprehension • Phonemic awareness • Initial and final consonant sounds • Consonant blends • Long and short vowel sounds • Fluency • Contextual analysis • Critical-thinking strategies
2 or 3	• Sight words • Meaning vocabulary • Oral language development • Comprehension • Contextual analysis • Long and short vowel sounds • Consonant blends and digraphs • Vowel principles • Structural analysis • Syllabication • Fluency • Critical-thinking strategies • Content-reading strategies
4 or 5	• Comprehension • Meaning vocabulary • Structural analysis • Fluency • Critical-thinking strategies • Content-reading strategies
6 and above	• Comprehension • Meaning vocabulary • Critical-thinking strategies • Content-reading strategies

Continuous Assessment and Reflection

Based on this initial assessment and priority decision-making, you are in position to design your instructional plans and teach. Yet, this initial assessment should not be the final word. It is important to realize that students' needs change and/or your initial assessment decisions may need to be adjusted after working with your student. Your initial assessment decisions should always be considered "best guesses." You must monitor and evaluate each day's lesson and make adjustments in future lessons if necessary. Each day's lesson becomes assessment material for tomorrow's lesson. Instructional modifications are hallmarks of effective reading instruction. This process helps you fulfill the following simple, but powerful statement: A major function of teaching reading is providing instruction to students based on their needs. The closer the match between your assessment results and your instruction, the greater the chance your students will be successful.

Model of Assessment-Instruction

Teachers use a great deal of energy in the teaching of reading. Whether teaching a specific skill or strategy, new vocabulary, or elements of a story, teachers are caught up with "doing." This is how it should be as long as continuous assessment and reflective thinking are linked to all instruction. Without this ongoing monitoring and reflective thinking, instruction becomes mindless drudgery for all concerned. The "doing" must fit into a conscious model relating assessment to instruction. Figure 2-2 represents this process.

Personal Observations: Teachers-in-Preparation

How does having students with unmet emotional needs affect your teaching?

"One of my students has low self-esteem and is lonely. He always looks down and is very sad. I must always be positive with him while at the same time try to improve his reading abilities. It is difficult."

"Dave is so competitive and is afraid to fail. I try to promote working at one's own pace and avoid competitive situations in the classroom."

"I have one student that has stayed back two times. He is embarrassed since his younger sister is in the same grade. He struggles with feelings of inadequacy and that his sister is better than him."

"This student wants love and affection—he is always looking for a hug and trying to touch me. It makes it very difficult for him to participate and stay focused on a topic."

"He has so little confidence in his academic abilities. He is very quiet most of the time and won't say an answer even if he knows it. He'll say the right word, but very quietly, and if asked to repeat it, he will say he forgot. He doesn't seem to think he can do things right, even though he is very smart and does very well. This affects

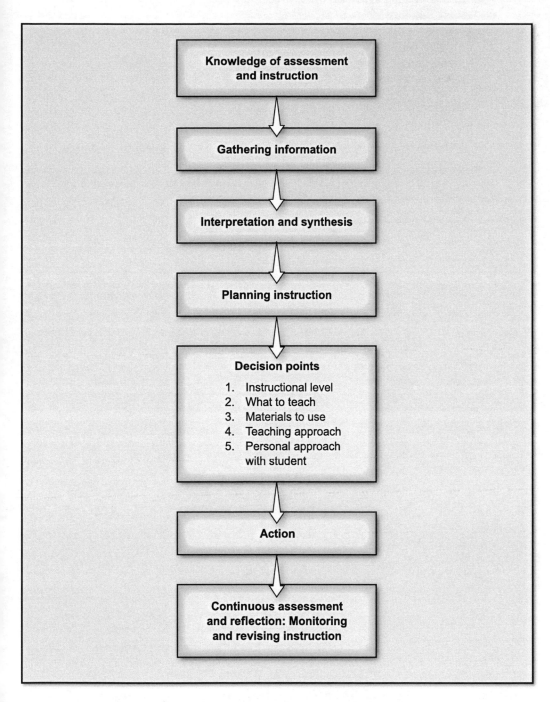

Figure 2-2 Assessment-Instruction Model

my teaching because I have to almost coax answers out of him and be extremely encouraging."

"Trisha seems to be lacking in love and affection. She gives me hugs each day. She always wants to hold my hand as we walk to and from the playground. She is also very talkative before and after our lessons: She just wants to tell me how her week was and what she's doing that weekend."

"I have a student who barely talked to other children and did not want to participate in activities for the first few weeks. We made sure that we called on her often and praised her contributions. Now, she volunteers all the time. She was asked if she wanted to change groups, but she wanted to stay with us. I think that she feels like she belongs in our group and needs that secure feeling of belonging."

Providing Differentiated Reading Instruction

Differentiated Instruction

A true story that is repeated many times in our schools involves individuals who try their hand at substitute teaching. Invariably for many of these people, substitute teaching does not last very long. The eye-opener, in addition to the obvious concern for discipline and management, is that students are different. This one fact is what makes teaching so intrinsically satisfying and at the same time so difficult. Students differ in a multitude of ways—in intelligence, social awareness, emotional maturity, psychological well-being, cultural backgrounds, thinking abilities, physical maturity, and current performance level or reading level, to name a few. What makes teaching reading so rewarding and challenging is that you must teach 20 to 30 different students, with different instructional needs, in one class at the same time. Thus, differentiated reading instruction is instruction that is adapted or modified to suit a student's current performance level and specific skill needs in reading, taking into account his or her emotional, personal, and cultural needs. The complexity of teaching reading is quickly realized when one tries to differentiate instruction in the classroom.

Realizing that your instruction will vary for different students depending on their needs, three overriding considerations in delivering differentiated instruction are: (1) opportunity to learn, (2) engaged time, and (3) balanced reading instruction. *Opportunity to learn* refers to immersing students in a literate environment, teaching them what they need to know to be successful readers, and providing multiple opportunities to apply their reading and writing skills and strategies in different reading situations. *Engaged time* means the type of classroom time in which there is a reasonably high level of student involvement or time-on-task. Research on teaching reading clearly shows that the more time students spend engaged in learning, the higher their achievement will be (Taylor et al., 1999). *Balanced reading instruction* means that a variety of teaching approaches (i.e., both explicit/direct and implicit/indirect), strategies, and materials are used to teach students how to read, coupled with opportunities for recreational reading. The emphasis is on the word *variety* because children are different in so many ways that one approach or strategy will not work equally well with every child. Effective teachers of reading focus on the five components of the reading process—phonemic awareness, phonics, fluency, vocabulary, and comprehension—and balance the teaching of these components based on their students' needs.

Grouping Students

Coupled with assessing each student's instructional level and determining specific strengths and weaknesses in understanding text, grouping students facilitates differentiated instruction in the classroom. Years ago, because of the large numbers of students in a class, grouping was thought a necessary evil. Today, the literature on effective teaching tells us that grouping for instruction is a means to capitalize on student differences and increase student achievement. Students learn from one another in a group and are more likely to work productively in groups than individually. Different types of groups—whole, small, partner, and individual—are based, in turn, on reading ability, interest, research, and cooperative learning. Effective teachers use a variety of groupings throughout the year to fit specific objectives and thus provide different instruction to different students. In this way, grouping is an integral part of providing differentiated instruction.

Teaching Reading

Good reading instruction doesn't "just happen" in the classroom but is the result of much teacher effort before students arrive. Your skill at planning will greatly affect both your success as a teacher and your students' learning. How you utilize time for differentiated instruction is the key. The proper use of instructional time cannot be "willed"; teachers must carefully plan how to achieve their instructional goals. Above all else, you must plan a reading program that is enjoyable for children; without this quality, all good intentions will not come to fruition.

From research on teaching reading (Rosenshine & Stevens, 1995), there has emerged a set of procedures that are effective in teaching specific reading skills and strategies to urban children (See Appendix B). These procedures—the explicit/direct instructional model—are embedded in the essential instructional framework and process that follow. Of course, you will need to modify any set of procedures based on your students, their grade and age, and their readiness for a particular instructional goal. Also, there are other important models of teaching to incorporate in your teaching, such as problem-solving and inquiry when fostering critical-thinking objectives.

The basic element of teaching is the individual lesson. This is the vehicle with which you teach students what they need to know. This is the means by which you advance your students' reading abilities. Upon this foundation, you can design a series of activities (or lessons) to attain instructional goals. The next four sections—"Pre-Planning Considerations," "Essential Instructional Components in the Reading Period," "Teacher Behaviors in Effective Reading Programs in Diverse Communities," and "The Necessity of Practice"—serve as your framework for teaching children to read.

Pre-Planning Considerations

Overall reminders:

- You must not only "be there" but also "be on" at the start of your reading lesson. That is, you must be ready to perform immediately.

- All materials must be ready before the start of the lesson.

- Always remember to make your instructional session enjoyable for you and your students.

Importance of Being a Self-Monitor

Each instructional plan is a blueprint for accomplishing instructional goals. Effective teachers self-monitor and reflect on their teaching, and they modify future lessons based on student responses. In essence, effective reading teachers always ask the question, "Why am I doing what I am doing?" In this way, you will grow in your ability and confidence to teach reading. The following are some of the essential questions teachers should ask themselves when implementing any reading lesson:

Before teaching:

- What prerequisite knowledge and skills do my students need to be successful with the present lesson?

- At what pace do I want to conduct the lesson? What will be the troublesome areas for my students?

- How will I tie the objectives of the lesson to previous learning of my students?

During teaching:

- Do my students understand the lesson objectives?

- Do my students need additional explanation and practice?

After teaching:

- Do I need to reteach a part of the lesson?

- Was the time too long or too short for the activity (or activities)?

- What checkup of mastery was made?

- What recommendations can I make to the parents for follow-up at home?

- What did I learn today that will be of help in my next lesson?

Essential Instructional Components in the Reading Period

The typical reading "period" is 1-1/2 hours in duration. While different published reading programs may dictate a specific cycle of activities, most reading programs contain similar emphases or components. Figure 3-1 shows those similar components that are covered during the block of time devoted to reading instruction. Depending on the particular grade, students, and instructional goals, you can expect to modify the components to fit your situation. A brief explanation of each of these components follows.

1. Readiness, Review, and Motivation

At the beginning of your lesson, have a conversation with your student(s) and share interests, weekly happenings, and events; review previous lessons; communicate to them the goals of the day; highlight one or two of the exciting things you have planned for them for the day; and tell them you expect them to do well in today's activities. If students are returning a book they read, talk about the book, discuss and summarize the book, and ask students whether or not they liked the book and why.

Figure 3-1 Instructional Components in the Reading Period

1. Readiness, review, and motivation

2. Vocabulary development

3. Thinking activity or
   Skill/strategy development or
   Fluency development or
   Coaching for understanding while reading

4. Guided reading and story retelling

5. Read aloud and independent reading and/or writing activities

6. Practice and reinforcement

7. Review

8. Evaluation and reflection

2. Vocabulary Development

For each lesson, teach new words—basic sight vocabulary words, meaning words, or both. Make sure to use each new word in real sentences (orally and/or written), and use these words throughout the lesson.

3. Thinking Activity

Teach a critical-thinking strategy (for example, hypothesizing, criticizing, inferring, looking for assumptions, or imagining) by explaining the strategy and providing supervised and independent activities. Use examples to discuss the strategy with the student, explain how it can be applied to everyday life, and how it might apply to the story to be read.   (or)

4. Skill/Strategy Development

Teach a word identification or comprehension skill or strategy using the explicit/direct instruction approach. Coach or assist students in applying the new skill or strategy as they read the story in guided reading.   (or)

5. Fluency Development

Provide students with fluency training, using the story previously read or another activity.   (or)

6. Coaching for Understanding While Reading

Provide students with open-ended sentences or short paragraphs, and ask them to write the missing part. This technique especially helps students who are word callers or verbalizers to think and to focus on the message *while* they are reading and not to solely focus on the words.

7. Guided Reading and Story Retelling

The centerpiece of your lesson is a story, and the manner or road map you use or follow to teach the story is called the Guided Reading Plan. The story should be on the student's instructional level. Follow the steps of preparation for reading (readiness, motivation, teaching difficult words, and setting a purpose), silent reading, and retelling the story and follow-up activities (answering the purpose-setting question, asking comprehension questions, summarizing the story, meaningful oral reading, and clarifying any points). The "retelling technique" is simply asking students to tell you about the story, discussing what happened first, second, third, and so forth. You can give hints along the way and use a story map or other visual format to illustrate the story structure and events. The vocabulary words previously taught and subsequent reading skills and strategies to be taught can be practiced and reinforced using this story.

8. Read Aloud and Independent Reading and/or Writing Activities

The ultimate goal of your lesson (and indeed the teaching of reading) is to foster in your students the desire and ability to read and enjoy books on their own. To this end, read a story or part of one to your students each day, and have your students complete an independent reading or writing activity (see chapter 16 for ideas).

9. Practice and Reinforcement

This component is optional, depending on time and students' needs. Play games with students to practice any new learnings from your lesson—vocabulary words, word identification, comprehension skill or strategy, or thinking strategy.

10. Review

Recap major goals for your lesson, and highlight progress made with each student.

11. Evaluation and Reflection

After each reading period, evaluate and reflect on your lesson to see if you achieved your prestated goals. Monitoring and evaluating both your effectiveness and your students' progress should be included in each part of your lesson. If students perform well, you can feel reasonably sure that your teaching was appropriate and that your students are ready for the next step. If students do not achieve the objectives of the lesson, you need to re-examine your teaching procedures and decide how to reteach the original learning objectives. This final reading session appraisal is the best feedback for both you and students because it lets you know how to teach tomorrow's lesson.

Teacher Behaviors in Effective Reading Programs in Diverse Communities

What considerations should guide your teaching in the classroom? How can you teach your lesson efficiently and effectively? The following teacher behaviors are specific courses of action to be implemented into your teaching lessons. These behaviors answer the question, "How do I focus my time and effort in teaching my lessons so as to enhance the quality of life and academic achievement of my students?"

Effective teachers:

- *Relate the culture, family, lives, and interests of students to the instructional goals; that is, use what students already know to teach them new skills, strategies, and content.*

   Examples:

   1. In a third-grade classroom, the teacher and students are reading a story about a character who lives in a predominately Spanish neighborhood. The character is bilingual and is constantly being asked to translate for her neighbors. The teacher can use this story to discuss what it feels like to be bilingual. She can ask students in class who are bilingual to share their experiences.

   2. Through parent conferences, invite parents to come into the classroom and share experiences from their background and culture. A parent who is originally from Greece, for example, could share information about Greek culture by bringing in traditional Greek food for students to sample, photos, or a picture book about Greece.

- *Use reading materials that relate to the cultural backgrounds of their students.*

   Examples:

   1. Use multicultural books for both instruction and for fostering independent reading habits.

2. Create language experience stories, and use the words in the story to develop vocabulary and comprehension.

- *Capitalize on students' comprehension abilities and background experiences.*

  Examples:

  1. Based on your interviews with your students, select multiethnic books to match your students' interests.

  2. Ask your students to write an individual story describing their favorite holiday and how it is celebrated with their family.

- *Use cooperative learning activities to foster academic achievement.*

  Examples:

  1. Pair students together to complete a crossword puzzle that highlights new words in a story.

  2. Pair students together to buddy-read. Each student takes turns reading a page in the story, and students use strategies to help each other decode words.

  3. Have students work together in groups or as partners to do a science experiment. Each person in the group has a responsibility, and group members work together to explain their thinking.

- *Promote intensive oral language development.*

  Examples:

  1. Use an abundance of group discussion for each lesson. Encourage students to explain their feelings and thinking.

  2. Provide meaningful, interactive, vocabulary word lessons. Encourage students to use vocabulary words in their discussions, and reward them when they are "caught" using a vocabulary word.

  3. Provide opportunities for students to act out stories, poems, and plays. Give students opportunities to plan, write, and perform orally in front of the class.

- *Make an extra effort to use students' existing knowledge and to build prior knowledge and background in getting students ready to read.*

  Examples:

  1. Use graphic organizers to review and build prior knowledge. One example is a K-W-L chart. Before starting a new unit, the teacher and students make a list of all of the things they know about the subject. This is the K column. They also start another column for what they want to learn. This is the W column. They can add to this as they move through the unit and more questions arise. Throughout the unit, the class also adds to an L column. This is the column where they write what they've learned. Several modifications can be made to this organizer. For example, an H column can be added for how students learned the information. The W column can be changed to N, for what do students need to learn.

  2. Use vocabulary words from the unit to introduce the new topic. Teach the vocabulary in a meaningful way, giving many examples and relating the words to students' lives.

3. Before starting a new unit, show students how to preview a chapter or book. Teach them how to read headings and subheadings, look for vocabulary words, read captions under the photos, and interpret graphs or diagrams. This will give students prior knowledge with the chapter or book and with the information.

- *Get students working on-task quickly at the beginning of the lesson.*

Examples:

1. Teach signals at the beginning of the year to indicate transition time. For example, at the beginning or at the end of each lesson, put up a signal that means "freeze." Every student then freezes for directions. The "give-me-five" signal also works. Hold up one hand and say, "Give me five." This is the signal for students to stop what they are doing and listen for instructions.

2. Sing songs to gain students' attention. Both older and younger students enjoy this. For example, you might sing the following to the tune of Frère Jacques:

   Are you talking? Are you talking?
   I hear you. I hear you.
   Show me how you're quiet.
   Show me how you're quiet.
   Right, right, now.
   Right, right, now.

- *Begin each separate lesson with a review of previous material, introduce and motivate each lesson to students, and specify the objectives of the lesson when appropriate.*

Examples:

1. State the objective and rationale for the lesson. Pose a question to students, asking them why they think this skill may be important.

2. Give students clear directions and expectations before each lesson.

3. Provide motivational incentives for students who are working on-task. These can be given individually or in groups. Students can work to earn extra privileges, such as lunch with you or extra free time.

- *Teach new skills and strategies by providing examples, modeling, and demonstrations followed by sufficient independent practice.*

Examples:

1. Display examples of the skill to be taught—for example, posters with the skill displayed or graphic organizers mapping the skill.

2. Use instructional music to help review and practice skills—for example, the ABC song set to music, or multiplication facts in the form of a rap song. Children respond well to music, and this is a fun way to practice skills.

- *Carry out each part of the lesson at a brisk pace, slowing only to improve or clarify student comprehension.*

Examples:

1. Use transition words, such as first we are going to do this, then we will do this, after that we will do this, and finally, to set the pace of the lesson.

2. Pause during the lesson to ask questions about the topic at hand. "Reporter questions," such as who, what, where, when, and why, work well for this purpose.

• *Summarize the main points of each lesson.*

Examples:

1. Work with students to complete graphic organizers to review material learned.

2. Ask students in groups to write a summary, draw an illustration, or answer comprehension questions that pertain to the lesson.

• *Provide constructive feedback regarding the correctness or incorrectness of student work/responses.*

Examples:

1. Review students' work. Use examples of correct work to set a standard and as an example of what work should look like.

2. Praise students in specific ways, giving students detailed examples of what they did correctly and how they could improve their work.

• *Design activities for students to share and use their bilingual abilities and knowledge.*

Examples:

1. Each week, ask a different student to bring in a poster board displaying items about the student and his or her family. The student presents the poster board and answers other students' questions about it. You might also ask the other students in the class to write the student presenter a letter, telling the student what they liked learning from the presentation.

2. When relevant to the lesson, ask students to translate whatever word or topic they are learning for the class. This should be done as an example for the class. This will also help relate the word or topic to other limited English-speaking students.

• *Expect students to achieve, and encourage and reward student effort in each activity.*

Examples:

1. Students of all ages enjoy personal attention and encouragement to achieve from the teacher. Provide motivational rewards for students who meet expectations. Additional rewards can be provided for students who exceed expectations. These rewards can be tangible, or they can be in the form of verbal praise. Some examples include positive notes to students and to parents, words of encouragement, a pat on the back, and a smile.

2. Incentive programs can make learning fun and are also a visual way for the student and the teacher to measure progress. Some examples include posters or charts highlighting progress and/or where students earn stickers for meeting goals.

The Necessity of Practice

The best readers are fluent and automatic; they read quickly, purposefully, and strategically to fulfill their goals without stopping to figure out how to pronounce words or to determine the significant details or main ideas. Such behaviors are not innate traits. This ability to read quickly, purposefully, and strategically without effort is the result of receiving much explicit/direct instruction from teachers and much varied, interesting, and meaningful practice on important reading skills and strategies from teachers. The same can be said for the star quarterback on the football team or the scratch, top-notch golfer. Each is able to perform his or her sport at a high level due to excellent instruction and practice.

The focus here is on practice. Many times, teachers shortchange this crucial step in the teaching-learning process. In life, as in learning to be an effective reader, there's no substitute for interesting and meaningful practice. Ben Hogan, the famous golfer, once said, "Every day you miss playing or practicing is one day longer it takes to be good." The same can be said regarding becoming a strategic reader. Without an abundance of practice, the best explicit/direct instruction is rendered useless, This practice must be done on a daily basis.

One possible explanation for students struggling in reading is that their skills and strategies were only "half-learned," and automaticity or complete transfer was not made. As a result of accumulating "half-learnings" throughout the grades, there are gaps that interfere with reading comprehension. Learning anything, and especially how to read, would be so easy if one only had to be shown how to perform a particular skill or strategy just once. For students to become fluent in their decoding abilities and master their comprehension skills and strategies, however, they not only need to be shown the "how-to's" but also need to practice and practice. There is no shortcut. Reading skills and strategies must be practiced in varied reading situations to achieve fluency and mastery. This fluency and mastery implies transfer; that is, students can now use their abilities in reading in new and different situations.

Practice must be:

- related specifically to what students need,

- on an appropriate reading level,

- abundant,

- interesting,

- monitored by the teacher by circling around the room and checking out how students are arriving at answers, and

- evaluated to determine the depth of students' understanding of the task.

If these conditions are met, students will become fluent and automatic readers. Without an abundance of meaningful practice, students will most likely fail and have lowered self-esteem. Many commercial and informal materials are available for practice. The crucial point is to use them effectively with your students.

Personal Observations: Students

What do you like about your teacher in school?

"She is very nice and does not scold me. She is respectful and fun."

"She is nice and lets us help people. She sings songs with us and lets us go to different centers."

"She teaches a lot to us, and she's fun and friendly. She does different activities and teaches us how to read a book."

"My teacher spends a lot of time helping me through stuff I don't understand."

"My teacher is nice to me and everyone else in my class."

"She is nice and laughs a lot. She gives us things that we can't do but then helps us do them. She helps us write because we don't know how."

"We have lots of fun everyday."

"She has long hair and beautiful eyes. She is great at reading and makes me laugh."

"I like my teacher because he gives us many chances to do things and he understands us. Most of all, he knows how it feels to have a bad day."

"He makes reading interesting and fun to be in class."

"She never picks favorites. She is a good explainer. She is also nice and loves to compliment us on our singing."

"She lets us read and is interested in the book I am reading."

Parents and Reading

Parental Influence on Children

Parents are their children's first teachers and, as such, have a tremendous influence on their children's reading development (Purcell-Gates, 1995; Waldbart, Meyers, & Meyers, 2006). What parents believe and do with their children during the first five years of life (especially in the areas of self-concept, background experiences, book sharing, and oral language development) is crucial to success in beginning reading in kindergarten and first grade. Parents also play an important role in what kind of readers their children ultimately become in school and later in life (National Institute of Child Health and Human Development, 2000). Because of this influence, classroom teachers need to accept the fact that parents are assets (rather than liabilities) to their children's learning. They should work to establish close ties with the parents, help the parents to become knowledgeable in the goals and content of the school's reading program, and partner with the parents in developing children's reading abilities. Stressing the need for an emphasis on parental participation and collaboration, Crawford and Zygouris-Coe (2005) state:

> Philosophically, teachers must first believe that the home life of children matters and that there is much to be gained from working with families to help children meet academic goals and develop a lifelong love of literacy. For teachers who have embraced these beliefs, the challenge then becomes one of welcoming families into the school and helping them to be involved with the educational process in meaningful ways. (p. 263)

Realities in Diverse Communities

No matter how important the involvement of parents is to student achievement or how many times it is highlighted in today's educational literature, involving parents is a challenge in diverse schools. Yet, it is worth all efforts to do so because most parents will cooperate with classrooms teachers if "invited" to do so. Most importantly, it is crucial never to doubt that parents in diverse communities value literacy. Baumann and Duffy (1997) report on research conducted for the National Reading Research Center (NRRC) that provided evidence that parents from a variety of cultural, ethnic, and linguistic backgrounds promote reading development in the home. The authors state, "We have also relearned that the stereotypes are wrong: Race, economics, and culture are inaccurate when it comes to predicting which families support their children's literacy development" (pp. 54–55). Once "invited" to share the responsibility of helping their children become literate, given information about present school reading practices, and shown how to teach specific reading skills and strategies, parents are eager to help their children improve their reading abilities and succeed in school. McCarthey (2000) reviewed the research literature on literacy practices at home and in school and concludes:

> Many of the studies conducted in the home environments of families from diverse backgrounds have challenged the myth that children from low-income backgrounds are not exposed to literacy materials and that parents are not concerned with their children's education. The studies also have demonstrated

that the type and amount to materials, the amount of time that parents and children engage in literacy-related activities, and the nature of the interactions are important factors in children's later success in school. (p. 151)

Many parents lead very stressful lives, balancing two or three jobs along with taking care of other family members, which leaves little time to devote to helping their children with schoolwork. Also, many parents (from all socioeconomic backgrounds) feel that they lack the skills to help their children (many have had unpleasant experiences themselves in school), that they do not know the reading curriculum of today's schools, and that, generally, their children's education is out of their hands. They may not realize how important it is for them to promote their children's reading abilities in the home. Classroom teachers need to understand and address all of these fears and perceptions in order to reverse the tide and have parents play an important part in their children's school success.

Remember, you will teach students with cultural backgrounds that are different from your own. This reality is a "given" in teaching. Another reality is that you will need to communicate and work with parents from different cultural backgrounds and who speak different languages. You will need to bridge the boundaries of race and culture in successfully partnering with parents of urban children. The following quote from the U.S. Commission on Civil Rights (1992) highlights this necessity and applies to many culturally diverse students and parents:

Many Asian American immigrant students and their parents arrive in this country with little background to help them understand American public school systems. Many have very little previous education, and what formal education they have received has been in a very different setting and in schools with a completely different structure and culture from those they find in America. Too often these students are dumped in our classrooms with little or no preparation, and their parents are given no help in understanding how our school system works and little opportunity to participate in making decisions about their children's education.

In addition to these understandings, many parents themselves may have difficulties in reading, and this likely will have direct effects on their children's reading development. Smith and Elish-Piper (2002) focus directly on the low levels of parental literacy and offer the following three reasons to be concerned with the whole area of adult literacy:

- Adults who struggle with literacy are likely to have children who will struggle with literacy.

- Parents with low literacy are less likely to help with their children's schoolwork, get involved in school activities, and communicate with their children's teachers.

- Adults with low literacy skills are more likely to have difficulty navigating the healthcare system and reading and understanding medical instructions; consequently, their children's health is likely to be affected.

Thus, while there are hurdles to overcome with all parents (regardless of socioeconomic level), it is imperative to realize that *parents in diverse communities value literacy, care very much about their children's reading progress, and want to know what they can do at home to increase their children's reading abilities.*

Help for Parents and Classroom Teachers

With the renewed emphasis on the importance of parental involvement, which is highlighted again and again in the educational literature, numerous sources today provide various ways for parents to foster their children's reading abilities. Libraries, local educational associations, professional organizations, journals and magazines, parent groups, independent agencies, university projects, state departments of education, and the U.S. Department of Education offer an array of print and nonprint resources to help parents and teachers play an important role in children's reading development. For example:

- The ERIC (Educational Resource Information Center, *http://www.eric.ed.gov*) Clearinghouse on Reading and Communication Skills at Indiana University (*http://reading.indiana.edu*) produce a multitude of publications for culturally diverse parents, including an audio-journal directed toward parents and children.

- The ERIC Clearinghouse on Elementary and Early Childhood Education and the National Parent Information Network (NPIN) at the University of Illinois at Urbana-Champaign (*http://npin.org*) have a variety of helpful resources for parents.

- The National Center for Family Literacy (*http://www.famlit.org* or call 1-877-326-5481) is a nonprofit organization that works to ensure that all families at the lowest ends of the literacy and economic continua have opportunities to improve their education and well-being through quality family literacy programs.

- The Partnership for Reading, a collaborative effort of the National Institute for Literacy (NIFL), the National Institute of Child Health and Human Development (NICHD), and the U.S. Department of Education, has published Put Reading First: Helping Your Child Learn to Read, a Parent Guide, which summarizes evidence-based reading research for parents and others with an interest in helping all people learn to read well. Copies of this brochure can be obtained from the NIFL by calling 1-800-228-8813, emailing *edpuborders@edpubs.org,* or downloading the document at *http://www.nifl.gov.*

- The U.S. Department of Education has published booklets for parents, including "Helping Your Child Become a Reader" and "Helping Your Child with Homework," in both English and Spanish. (*http://www.nochildleftbehind.gov* or call in request toll-free: 1-877-433-7827).

- The National Child Care Information Center (NCCIC) (*http://nccic.acf.hhs.gov*) is a national clearinghouse and technical assistance center linking parents, providers, policy-makers, researchers, and the public to early care and education information. NCCIC responds to requests from parents, child-care providers and other early education professionals, researchers, policy-makers, national organizations, businesses, and the general public on various child-care topics, including reading development. INCCIC's Online Library is the largest collection of summaries and links to full-text publications about child care and early childhood education. The following is a sample of NCCIC publications that have information for early childhood educators and parents about literacy development in young children:

  - *A Guide to Early Literacy in Child Care: Learning to Read and Write Begins at Birth* (2004), by Child Care Aware, is a brochure for parents and caregivers that gives information on how to build young children's early reading and writing skills. It also provides an Early Literacy Child-Care Checklist to help parents evaluate the early literacy materials that caregivers offer. This resource is available in English on the Internet at *http://www.childcareaware.org/en/ tools/pubs/pdf/112e.pdf* and in Spanish (Guia del alfabetismo temprano en el ambiente de cuidado de ninos: El aprender a leer y escribir comienza al nacer) at *http://www.childcareaware.org/en/tools/pubs/pdf/112s.pdf.*

- "Helping Your Child Go Places through Literacy" (2004), *The Daily Parent,* Vol. 15, prepared by the National Association of Child Care Resource and Referral Agencies (NACCRRA), presents strategies for parents to use with their infants, toddlers, preschoolers, and school-age children that will foster reading, writing, and speaking well. This resource is available on the Internet at *http://www.childcareaware.org/en/dailyparent/vol15/.*

- *A Child Becomes a Reader: Proven Ideas for Parents from Research—Birth through Preschool* (2003), by Bonnie B. Armbruster, Fran Lehr, and Jean Osborn, National Institute for Literacy, presents ideas from research on how to help children become good readers and writers and describes characteristics of effective literacy programs in child-care centers, preschools, and classrooms. Two lists of reading accomplishments that can be expected for a child by 3 years of age and by 5 years of age are outlined, based on research in the fields of reading, early childhood education, and child development. Helpful terms to know, suggested reading, and a list of resources for parents and caregivers are provided. This resource is available on the Internet at *http://www.nifl.gov/ partnershipforreading/publications/earlychildhood.html.*

- *Reading Tips for Parents* (May 2003), by the U.S. Department of Education, offers a host of tips for parents who wish to read for and with their children. The brochure first provides some general tips, such as "Read aloud at least 15 minutes a day to your child," and "Make a special place in your home where your child can read and write." It then describes developmental stages for children under 2 years of age and offers targeted techniques to use with children under 2 years. It does the same for toddlers 2–3 years old, preschoolers 3–4 years old, and for kindergartners 5–6 years old. This resource is available in English on the Internet at *http://www.ed.gov/parents/read/ resources/readingtips/readingtips.pdf* and in Spanish (*Consejos practicos para los padres sobre la lectura*) at *http://www.ed.gov/espanol/parents/read/ resources/sobrelecture/sobrelecture.pdf.*

- *Put Reading First: Helping Your Child Learn to Read: A Parent Guide: Preschool through Grade 3* (2001), published by The Partnership for Reading, a collaborative effort of the National Institute for Literacy (NIFL), the National Institute of Child Health and Human Development (NICHD), and the U.S. Department of Education, is designed for parents of young children. It describes the kinds of early literacy activities that should take place at school and at home to help children learn to read successfully. These reading activities are broken down into three categories: (1) children who are just beginning to learn to read, (2) children who are just beginning to read, and (3) children who are reading. It is emphasized that learning to read takes more practice than children get during the school day. It is based on the findings of the

National Reading Panel. This resource is available in English on the Internet at *http://www.nifl.gov/partnershipforreading/publications/Parent_br.pdf*. This resource is also available in Spanish (*La Lectura es lo Primero*) at *http://www. nifl.gov/partnershipforreading/publications/pdf/PRF_espan_.pdf*.

- *Starting Out Right: A Guide to Promoting Children's Reading Success* (1999), by M. Susan Burns, Peg Griffin, and Catherine E. Snow, National Academy Press, identifies questions and explores answers regarding early literacy development, drawing upon the *Preventing Reading Difficulties in Young Children* study. Guidance is provided about the key elements children need to succeed in reading; what parents and caregivers can provide to prepare children for reading instruction upon entering school; what language and literacy concepts to include in reading instruction; how reading difficulties can be prevented; and what to ask school boards, principals, and policy-makers regarding early reading instruction. In addition, the book offers checklists of specific reading accomplishments from preschool through 3rd grade, 55 literacy activities, a list of 100 recommended children's books, a guide to computer software and CD-ROMs, and a list of Internet resources. This resource is available on the Internet at *http://www.nap.edu/books/0309064104/html*.

- Florida Online Reading Professional Development (FOR-PD) is a large-scale online staff development project designed to help teachers improve reading instruction for learners in grades preK–12. The focus of FOR-PD's literacy newsletter for October 2006 was on family literacy (available at *http://www.itrc.ucf.edu/forpd/newsletter/FLN200610.html*).

- The Illinois Early Learning Project (*http://illinoisearlylearninj.org/*) publishes *Tip Sheets* (short handouts with practical information for parents and teachers) in English, Spanish, and Polish on a variety of early literacy topics, such as "Sharing Books with Your Toddler," "Things to Do While You're Waiting: Language and Literacy," and "Young Authors at Work: Literature Response Journals."

- The SouthEast Initiatives Regional Technology in Education Consortium (SEIR*TEC, *http://www.seirtec.org/*) is a group of national, regional, and university-based organizations dedicated to promoting the use of technology to improve teaching and learning. SEIR*TEC provides online "Reading Resources for Parents of Preschool Children" and "Reading Resources for Parents," which address the five essential components of reading identified by the National Reading Panel—phonemic awareness, phonics, fluency, vocabulary, and comprehension. In addition, they have online reading resources for parents of children in grades K–3 and 4–6, middle school, and high school.

- The Florida Literacy and Reading Excellence (FLaRE) project at the University of Central Florida (*http://flare.ucf.edu*) is the literacy center for professional development currently operating as a part of the Just Read, Florida! Initiative. This project disseminates information about K–12 literacy instruction and assessment statewide, and provides professional development for reading teachers, reading coaches, and district personnel. Figures 4-1 and 4-2 present some excellent suggestions to teachers by Zygouris-Coe (2006) from the FLaRE project for strengthening the school-family literacy connection.

- The prestigious Center for the Study of Reading at the University of Illinois has made excellent suggestions for parents to help their children become better readers—see Figure 4-3. These suggestions could be utilized as a handout at parent conferences

Culturally Sensitive Strategies for Fostering Parental Involvement

Just as it is important to "read" or know all you can about your children to successfully teach them, it is equally important to "read" or know your children's families, backgrounds, and cultures when working with parents. As a reading teacher, this knowledge will help you design an effective strategy to identify with parents and their needs, communicate your commitment to their children, and express your interest in the parents' involvement in helping their children to grow in their reading abilities. The following expanded list of strategies (Blair, 2003, pp. 38–39) illuminates the importance of knowing your parents and developing a partnership with them to promote reading development both at school and in the home:

- Learn about your parents' cultures and backgrounds.

- Communicate your sincere interest in their child and your willingness to help them as much as possible in having their child be a success in school.

Figure 4-1 How to Communicate Effectively with Families

Communicating effectively with families is a key factor in helping children succeed in school. Teachers and parents need to work together to support students in becoming strategic learners and readers. The following are helpful suggestions for teachers:

1. Keep communication simple, consistent, practical, warm, and personal.

2. Call parents to introduce yourself at the beginning of the year, and later on throughout the year to report student progress, discuss problems, or just to find out how you can best serve the family's school needs.

3. Write personal notes to invite parents to school or class events.

4. Keep an informal record of your contacts with families. This will help you to keep track of situations or progress.

5. Do "Get to Know You and Your Family" activities. This will help you get relevant information about each student and his or her family.

6. Send weekly or monthly newsletters home. Inform parents about school/class events, report card days, parent conferences, trips, and classes, or offer tips for test preparation, tips for parents, etc.

7. Have open house days, and invite all parents to attend.

8. Write positive comments on students' work to recognize progress. Provide certificates or stickers for student successes, and send them home for parents to see.

Source: Zygouris-Coe, 2006.

Figure 4-2 How to Strengthen School and Home Connections

The following is a summary of core suggestions for creating partnerships among school, parents, and community:

1. Share information with parents on the benefits of regular reading to children's literacy development.

2. Allow children, parents, and caregivers to borrow books from the classroom or school library.

3. Discuss the benefits of public libraries, how to use them, and how to benefit from programs that may be available for storytelling, reading, or parenting.

4. Recruit high school, college, and community volunteers to read to children in the school library during parent meetings. Free child care can improve parent attendance.

5. Invite parents to become involved in your classroom and at school.

6. Create a homework club to provide help to students and their parents.

7. Technology classes for parents and students can enhance parental involvement in the school and introduce parents to new ways of learning. Parents can acquire word processing skills, while their children receive hands-on experience with computers.

Source: Zygouris-Coe, 2006.

Figure 4-3 How Parents Can Help Their Children Become Better Readers

1. *Help your children acquire a wide range of knowledge.* When you take your children on shopping trips, walks in the park, and visits to zoos and museums, you help give them the important background knowledge they will need as they learn to read school textbooks. Your children's ability to understand even simple stories can depend upon their having both common and not-so-common knowledge.

2. *Talk with your children about their experiences.* When you talk with your children about their experiences, you help them learn new words and understand what these new words mean. Talking with children also helps them learn from their experiences and use this new knowledge to understand what they are reading. As a result, they will better understand what they are reading.

3. *Encourage your children to think about events.* Ask your children to describe events; this makes them reflect upon experiences and helps them learn to give good descriptions and tell complete stories. These activities help your children learn about how stories are written and better understand what they are reading.

4. *Read aloud to your children.* Reading aloud is probably the single most important activity you can do to encourage your children's success as readers. It is an especially important activity during the preschool years. When you read lots of stories to your children, and look at lots of picture books with them, you are helping them build the store of knowledge they will use when they begin to read in school. The benefits of reading aloud are greatest when you encourage your children to participate in activity by identifying letters and words and talking about the story and the meaning of words.

5. *Provide your preschool children with writing materials.* Writing is an important way for your children to learn about letters and words. Children are often very

(Continued)

Figure 4-3 *(Continued)*

eager to learn how to write, and you can encourage them by having paper and pencils or crayons in your home and helping them when they start drawing letters. Even when your children are too young to hold a pencil or crayon, you can use devices such as magnetic boards and letters to help them learn about letters and words.

6. *Encourage your children to watch TV programs that have educational value.* Watching television programs that teach about reading and language can have a positive effect on your children's learning. You can make sure they watch these programs regularly. You can also help them learn from these programs by asking questions about the shows and relating what they are seeing to other situations and experiences.

7. *Monitor how much TV your children watch.* Watching quality television programs up to about 10 hours a week can have a slightly positive effect on you children's achievement in school, including their reading achievement. As the number of hours of viewing per week increases, however, TV watching becomes a negative influence on your children's schoolwork. Most children who watch television 20 or more hours a week don't do well in school.

8. *Monitor your children's school performance.* When you visit your children's teachers, observe their classrooms, find out about the reading programs in their schools, and participate in home-school programs, you can get a good idea of how your children are doing in school and how you can help them become better students. Research shows that children tend to be more successful readers when their parents have an accurate view of their schoolwork.

9. *Encourage your children to read independently.* The amount of reading your children do outside of school influences how well they will read in school. Must American children don't read very much during their free time. One of your top priorities as a parent should be to encourage your children to spend more time reading. You can help them read more by having plenty of books in your home and visiting the library regularly.

10. *Continue your personal involvement in your children's growth as readers.* Set a good example for your children by reading newspapers, magazines, and books. Suggest reading as a leisure-time activity, and make sure your children have time for reading. You may want, for example, to establish a bedtime hour after which reading is the only activity permitted other than going to sleep.

Source: From "10 Ways to Help Your Children Become Better Readers," Center for the Study of Reading, University of Illinois, n.d.

- Arrange for home visits (along with supporting bilingual personnel if necessary).

- Ask the parents about their child's interests and background experiences—any information that might help you understand their child.

- Share with parents the goals and content of the school's reading program.

- Explain to parents the importance of becoming a reading family and setting aside time each day for reading.

- Prepare home learning kits with books, activities, games, and descriptions of strategies for parents to use in helping their children learn (both in their native language and in English).

- Discuss with parents their child's strengths and the areas in which their child needs improvement. Emphasize that parents and teachers together can be successful in improving their child's reading abilities.

- Show parents how they can assist their children with their homework. Be clear and avoid educational jargon.

- Prepare a newsletter in English and in the parents' native language to keep parents involved and informed. Many times PTA members or school employees can help in translating ideas. When sending a note home, consult the website *http:// freetranslation.com* for help in sending the note in different languages (just type your note, and it will be translated into many different languages).

- When planning a school meeting, design welcoming signs in the parents' language, and plan for another person to be a translator.

- In a parent-teacher conference, explain to parents how to interpret a reading progress form.

- Share with parents how important it is to talk to their children about school and school events. Also, encourage grandparents to discuss happenings at school with their grandchildren.

- Encourage parents to provide learning experiences outside of school. Museums, libraries, movies, zoos, wildlife refuges, parks, and universities offer good learning experiences.

- Encourage parents to display their child's schoolwork in a prominent place in the home to make the child feel good about himself or herself.

- Invite parents to assist in class and on school projects.

- Provide parents with a listing of community agencies that may offer training to parents to increase their involvement in the schools and to improve their child's educational opportunities.

- Recommend that parent-teacher meetings be held at neighborhood community centers.

Parental Expectations

Expectations—of both teachers and parents—are powerful indicators of student learning. Many times, parents do not realize how important it is for them to hold high expectations for their children concerning their schoolwork and to communicate these expectations to their children. Expectations can influence student learning. Students often sense what is expected of them and behave accordingly. Thus, expectations can become a self-fulfilling prophecy. Effective teachers believe that their students can and will learn, and they communicate this expectation to them. Likewise, parents need to do the same. Figure 4-4 is a suggested handout for parents on how they can communicate high expectations to their children.

Personal Observations: Parents

What is your first memory of learning to read?

"I don't remember basic reading instruction, but I do remember sitting on the floor while my teacher read the class a story. I always looked forward to that time of day. It was as though I was in a different world."

It is important that you not only want your children to be good readers but that you also tell your children that you "expect" them to do well in school and in learning to read. Your expectations about how well your children can and should perform in school will have a powerful effect on their learning. You want to hold high expectations for your children and communicate these expectations to them. So, how can you make sure that you are holding and communicating high expectations to your children? Here are a few tips:

- Tell your children each day that you have faith in them, that they are improving, and that they will be successful in school that very day.

- In the evening, ask your children about the day, and praise them for listening to their teacher and working hard in school. Even on those days when everything did not go well in school, remind your children that we all have bad days but that the important thing is that they are doing well, are improving, and that you are proud of their efforts and of them.

- Monitor your children's homework each day, and praise them for their good work. If your children are experiencing a problem with an assignment, sit down with them and try to help.

- Have a special interest in "attention to detail." Ask your children what book they are reading in class and what reading skills they are learning in school. Have your children show you their schoolwork, and check to see if they are completing the work neatly and completely. Tell them that you can tell they are improving in reading and how smart they are.

- Be "excited" about your children reading books. Ask them to tell you about the books they are reading each day.

- Make a progress chart listing each book your children read, and attach it to the refrigerator.

- At the end of each week, talk to your children about school and what new things they learned. Tell them what a great week they had and that you are proud of them.

Figure 4-4 Communicating High Expectations to Your Children

"My first memory of reading was with my Mom trying to show me that reading was from left to right and not from right to left. I remember crying, and the tears fell all over my reading book, and the dark letters began to fade. My Mom, a single Mom, was frustrated but in one night, I learned how to read from left to right. With lots of practice with my Mom, I got better and better and now I love to read."

"Being read to by my mother and her showing me words for me to repeat back to her."

What does being able to read mean to you? (Or how important is it for you to be able to read?)

"Everything, without reading you cannot function properly. Reading is the key to success and understanding. It is the foundation for the rest of your future as an adult."

"I am literate, which is a gift that I thank God for each day. I do not take reading for granted and try to improve in my vocabulary and understanding."

"Being able to read opens the door to a lifetime of learning. Reading will take you to places that you may never get to in life. What a great experience we get, when we read."

"Reading is my time to get information."

"As a grandmother and having the custody, I can help my grandchild to read and be successful in life. Nobody can take away the knowledge you get when you read. I love to read."

"Reading is important because it is the key to success. Without reading we would have to depend only on TV, radio, and other people. By being able to read, we are independent and more educated."

"Being able to read means a lot to me because it follows you all of your life. It makes it a lot easier to understand what's going on in the world. People who struggle or have issues with reading have it hard."

"Being able to read is very important to me. It enables me to perform my daily job (employment). It also makes it easier to help my children with schoolwork and the extra activities they are involved with at school."

"To me, reading means being able to function in society. Reading is important because I need to read the newspaper, street signs, food labels, and directions to different places. Without reading, it would be difficult to survive. Also, I have a child who finds it difficult to read, and I need to be able to help him."

"Reading is so important because if you do not know how to read, you can't do anything in this world."

Critical Teaching Performance Areas:
Capsule Summaries

Communicating High Teacher Expectations

5

What It Is and What Research Can Tell Us

Teacher expectations are "the mental set through which teachers filter perceptions of individual student performance" (Harris & Hodges, 1995, p. 252). A teacher's attitudes and expectations about how well a student can and should perform on a given task can have a powerful effect on the eventual outcome. Effective reading teachers hold high academic expectations for their students and communicate these high expectations to students. Increased student achievement and motivation are linked to high teacher expectations (Johnson et al., 2000). Low teacher expectations are likely to interfere with students successfully learning to read. In addition, effective reading teachers believe in themselves and their abilities, and feel it is their responsibility whether or not their students learn. Teachers who believe in both their students and themselves offer more effective instruction than teachers who do not hold these beliefs.

Teacher Behaviors

- Base instructional decisions on assessment information.

- Design activities so all students are involved and participate in learning.

- Select reading materials that reflect students' cultural heritage, backgrounds, and interests.

- Avoid sending negative messages regarding student ability.

- Communicate to all students both publicly and privately that you expect them to meet high standards in the classroom.

- Monitor student work and give timely feedback.

Teaching Strategies

1. *Get to know your students on a personal level*—what makes them tick and their interests (use the interest inventory in Figure 2-1 in Chapter 2 as a starting point), backgrounds, and preferred learning activities. Knowing your students will help you to project and communicate high expectations and to assume personal responsibility for every student's progress. Communicate this interest in your students daily, and convince them that they will be successful in your classroom. The best teaching techniques and materials are lost if not implemented in a positive atmosphere in which each child is expected to succeed.

2. *Design daily lessons so that all students are involved in every activity, and no one is left out.* Nothing (outside of direct criticism in front of their peers) causes more emotional conflict for students than to feel excluded in the classroom. When possible, create a supportive, caring atmosphere using cooperative grouping in which students foster positive peer relationships and are actively involved in the lesson.

3. *Monitor learning activities for students experiencing difficulties in reading.* Ask yourself, "Am I providing each student in my class (even those experiencing difficulty) with varied experiences in each of the major components of literacy

growth?" It is essential that you check yourself and your program to ensure that you provide a balanced reading program for all students in your class.

4. *Have a special interest in "attention to detail."* Successful reading teachers are goal oriented. They base their instruction for every student on specific information gleaned from the assessment process. Effective reading teachers know that students do not learn to read through osmosis but through carefully planned instruction based on specific, individual needs. Always be ready to answer the question, "Why are you doing what you are doing?" with specific educational information to justify your instructional decisions.

Emphasizing Oral Language Development

What It Is and What Research Can Tell Us

Oral language is speech representing accepted symbols and meanings. It is comprised of an individual's listening and speaking abilities. Although many factors contribute to the lack of reading achievement in diverse populations, many children come to school with basic oral language deficiencies in standard or mainstreamed dialect, the language of instruction in our schools. Remember, children bring their culture and family with them to school, and language and communication are influenced by one's culture. It is important to realize that nonmainstream children have oral language strengths, and reading instruction should capitalize on them, while at the same time, modeling and developing the mainstream dialect. Thus, you must respect a child's language and use it as a launching pad for oral language activities. A student's oral language ability is related to success in reading because reading development and oral language development are interdependent processes. Oral language development is directly related to the ability to read, for in oral language, the symbols are spoken, and in reading, they are written. The ability to talk about one's experiences is a foundation for learning to read and understanding text. Children cannot become successful in understanding written text if they cannot understand the spoken words. Anderson et al. (1985) highlight the importance of oral language very effectively in the classic text *Becoming a Nation of Readers: The Report of the Commission on Reading* when they state:

> Reading instruction builds especially on oral language. If this foundation is weak, progress in reading will be slow and uncertain. Children must have at least a basic vocabulary, a reasonable range of knowledge about the world around them and the ability to talk about their knowledge. These abilities form the basis for comprehending text. (p. 30)

Oral language development is especially important for children who come to school speaking a dialect or whose native language is not English. Many times, students' exposure to the type of oral language used in schools is at odds with their home language. It is widely documented that many poor, urban children come to school lagging behind in oral language development (West, Denton, & Germino-Hauskin, 2000). Oral language is an area that needs constant instruction and nourishment in all classrooms, but especially with diverse populations. Anderson et al. (1985) agree and state:

> Oral language experience in the classroom is especially important for children who have not grown up with oral language that resembles the language of schools and books. (p. 30)

Teacher Behaviors

- Design activities so all students are involved and participate in language experiences, including speaking, listening, writing, and reading.

- Explicitly/directly teach and practice the language and sentence structures of oral language.

- Design activities for students to share and use their bilingual and dialectal abilities and knowledge.

- Read interactively with students stories that reflect students' cultural heritage, backgrounds, and interests.

Teaching Strategies

1. *Talk to and listen to your students*—about everything (e.g., weekend happenings for the students and yourself, community center events, family parties, the weather, people in the news, students' favorite music and TV programs, a review of the school day, and so forth). Discuss with your students different ways of orally communicating ideas and everyday functions.

2. *Read books aloud to your students,* and make the experience as "interactive" as possible. Discuss the pictures and main characters, make predictions together, discuss the sequence of events after reading, and ask students their opinion of the story.

3. *Use "environmental print,"* such as road signs, bumper stickers, grocery labels, fast-food signs, community center flyers, theme park advertisements, and so forth, to increase oral language abilities.

4. *Take your students on trips and excursions to places of interest.* Upon returning, discuss the trips with the students and make stories about them.

5. *Use videos to expand students' horizons and oral language abilities.* Discuss the videos and incorporate art and music projects when applicable.

6. *Have students participate in Show and Tell,* an age-old activity that is excellent for practicing oral communication and connecting the classroom to the home.

7. *Brainstorm with students* to come up with words comprising general categories, such as shapes, colors, questions, happy words, and so forth, for help in oral communication.

8. *Use plays, puppet shows, pantomime, and other dramatic activities to extend oral language development.*

9. *Show students picture dictionaries and illustrated books, and discuss interesting topics and words.* Encourage students to tell you about a picture or to tell you a story about the word or picture.

10. *Tell students a story, and have them interact with you about the sequence of events in the story.*

11. *Use multimedia computer software and audio books to experience language.*

12. *Experiment with choral speaking,* which involves more than one person speaking as one. There are many different types of choral speaking: unison reading of a few sentences or a short story (and perhaps clapping out the rhythm), different groups of students reading different lines in a story, or students reading the refrain of a poem.

13. *Role-play* various telephone calls to model effective oral language use.

14. *Explore wordless books,* which provide excellent opportunities for students to discuss the plot, characters, and sequence of events; predict future events; and talk about the feelings of the characters.

15. *Provide explicit/direct explanations* to students on various aspects of the social functions of language, such as how to ask questions, give directions, express opinions, and so forth.

16. *Directly and indirectly focus on language acquisition* of mainstream oral language and sentence structures throughout the day. An excellent program for students with low oral language and literacy development is the *Oracy Instructional Guide,* developed by Lance Gentile (2004). This is an excellent, interactive program that uses the components of repeated sentences and sentence transformations, story reconstruction and narrative comprehension, picture drawing with narration, and critical dialogues about stories.

17. *Use the language experience approach (LEA),* which is a language arts approach to the teaching of reading, using the child's own language. LEA presents reading as a natural extension of speaking. The most common activity is the student's dictation of his or her experiences to the teacher. The teacher writes down the student's story on a poster board (called an experience chart). After writing down the student's oral responses exactly as stated and finishing the story, the teacher gradually and respectfully changes the oral language into mainstreamed or standard dialect with students. These stories are then used to teach specific reading skills and strategies. The advantages of LEA are many and include:

- Helps in explaining to students the relation of their oral language to written material

- Helps foster the development of formal, standard English

- Illustrates the close connection between what students say and what they will read

- Recognizes and respects children's oral language in creating reading material

- Helps in showing students that reading is useful

- Provides high motivation to learn by using students' own language in creating reading material

Developing Prior Knowledge

What It Is and What Research Can Tell Us

Prior knowledge is understanding that comes from previous experience. Readers comprehend the meaning of what they read by relating new information to what they already know—their background knowledge or their prior knowledge. Readers make connections between what they already know (their understandings from previous experience) and the ideas presented in the text. Thus, how well students comprehend what they read depends in large part on their prior knowledge of the topic (Alexander and Jetton, 2000). Another way of stating this is: "The more you know about a topic before you read it, the more you will comprehend and learn while you read it."

The first practical teaching implication related to prior knowledge is that teachers need to help students connect to the text to be read by relating the upcoming new information to what students already know about the topic. A second practical implication of the importance of prior knowledge is ensuring that students have the "prerequisite" knowledge to be successful with new material.

Teacher Behaviors

- Identify the knowledge and skills students need to be successful with the intended learning goal.

- Model or demonstrate for students what you know about a particular topic, and tell students that this establishes a mind-set of familiarity before they read.

- Give students a list of questions about what they will read; the questions will serve as purposes/predictions to guide their reading.

- Explain new information about a topic before students read.

- Build background knowledge on a topic to use in future reading experiences.

Teaching Strategies

1. *Examine visual aids.* This technique involves looking at visual aids before reading and asking students appropriate questions to trigger information already known and to develop new knowledge. Visual aids include not only pictures, but also maps, charts, diagrams, time lines, and graphs. Direct students' attention to each visual aid in the text to be read, and model for them how to closely analyze each visual aid. The old saying, "A picture is worth a thousand words," is appropriate here. Together with students, ask questions about the visual aids, using the "reporter questions" of *who, what, where, when, why*, and *how*. Using a chart, poster board, or chalkboard, write down answers to these "reporter questions." Next, discuss each entry in the chart, and ask students probing questions, such as "Can you tell me more?" "What does this mean to you?" "Do you agree? Disagree?" "What assumptions are you making?" and "Are you sure you mean what you said?" After discussing the answers

to the "reporter questions" but before students actually read the text, ask students what they want to know further on this topic or what they think the text will be about.

2. *Brainstorm a topic.* As a prereading strategy, brainstorm the topic of a story or chapter with students. Write all of their responses on the chalkboard under the main topic. Discuss the students' various responses, and use a visual format such as a flowchart or wheel with spokes to organize everything students came up with while brainstorming. Use this visual format as a postreading technique with your students for further amplification and discussion.

3. *Create a semantic map.* A semantic map is a visual technique for reviewing key vocabulary in an upcoming story or chapter and for teaching new vocabulary or concepts by showing the relationships among words. By introducing and discussing key vocabulary, you help students to review what they already know about a topic and to more easily learn new words on the same topic. To construct a semantic map, select a key word or concept from an upcoming story or chapter, and brainstorm related words to form various categories. Together, you and your students can design a semantic map before reading a selection and then revise the map after reading by making additions and deletions. The semantic map is the key factor in reviewing prior knowledge and developing new information on the topic at hand. An example of a semantic map is provided in Figure 7-1.

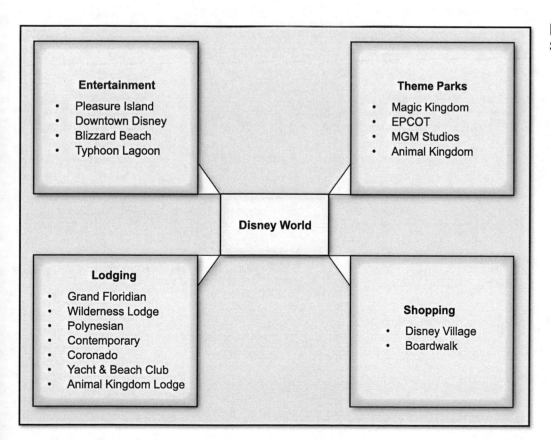

Figure 7-1 Example of a Semantic Map

Teaching Phonemic Awareness

What It Is and What Research Can Tell Us

Phonemic awareness is the understanding that words in our language are made up of a sequence of individual, connected sounds or phonemes. A phoneme is a speech sound. Students with this understanding can identify sounds and manipulate them. Heilman (2006) lists the following understandings a child can exhibit when this ability is achieved:

- Words have small sounds that can be pulled apart and put back together.

- Sounds in words have a specific order (first, middle, and final).

- Sounds in words can be counted.

- Sounds in words can be moved, removed, or replaced to make new words.

- Several sounds can be represented by different letters. (p. 29)

Phonemic awareness is a major predictor of becoming a successful reader in not only first grade but beyond (National Institute of Child Health and Human Development, 2000). This ability to hear individual sounds, discriminate among them, and manipulate them is the foundation for learning the sound/symbol relationships of English.

Many students have little difficulty with phonemic awareness. Being read to and informally playing with words in the home and in preschools teaches students about sounds and letters. However, first-graders lacking phonemic awareness have extreme difficulty with traditional phonics instruction and need a blend of implicit/indirect instruction and explicit/direct instruction to promote its development.

Teacher Behaviors

- Provide both implicit/indirect instruction and explicit/direct instruction to teach specific aspects of phonemic awareness.

- Provide an abundance of meaningful practice to promote student awareness and mastery.

- Monitor student progress.

Teaching Strategies

1. *Engage in implicit/indirect instruction,* and informally play with sounds by singing songs, playing rhyming games, and reading tongue twisters and books that rhyme or feature alliteration (i.e., contain words that begin with the same sound). Discuss the sounds in the rhyming books, songs, tongue twisters, and games, and have students say them. Play around with sounds with students by asking questions such as, "What words rhyme?" "What is the first sound of all the words in our song or book?" "Can you give me another word with the same sound?" Ask students to match sounds to various objects and words in sentences and stories.

2. *Employ explicit/direct instruction,* and practice with sounds and their components in the following areas:

- *Phoneme substitution.* Examples: Ask students to say the word *TIN* and to then indicate what the word would say if the sound of /t/ is replaced with the sound of /p/. Do the same with the word *BOOK,* where the beginning sound of /b/ is replaced with /t/.

- *Phoneme isolation.* Examples: Ask students to listen to the word *TOP* and to tell you where in the word they hear the sound of /t/. Or in the word *BLOSSOM,* where do they hear the sound of /s/? Or in the word *RADIO,* where do they hear the sound of /o/?

- *Phoneme deletion.* Examples: Ask students to say the word *AIRPLANE* and to then say the word without saying *PLANE.* Then ask students to say the word *FARM* and then to say the word without saying /f/, or to say the word *BOLD* and then to say the word without the /b/.

- *Phoneme segmentation.* Examples: Ask students to say a word one sound at a time, as in the word *NO* (n-oh) or *HOT* (h-o-t).

- *Blending words.* Examples: Pronounce words in small parts, such as *s-un* and *can-dee,* and ask students to put the parts together and pronounce the whole word.

Activities

- **Recognizing words with the same sound.** Give students a set of words—for example, *cat, dog,* and *cake.* Ask students to say the words aloud. Then have students say the words that have the same beginning sound. You may want to ask students to tell/say what the beginning sound is. Do this several different times.

- **Isolating sounds.** Show students a list of words. Focus on one word at a time. For example, show the word *dog,* and ask students to say the beginning sound of the word. You can do this with the first and last sounds in a word. Be sure you do this several times with other words.

- **Phoneme segmentation.** In this activity, you want students to break a word into its separate sounds, saying each sound as they tap out or count it. Then they will write and read the word. For example, ask students how many sounds are in the word *dog*? Students then tap out or count out each sound in *dog.* Then ask students to write the sounds in *dog.* After students write the sounds out, have them say the word again.

- **Phoneme blending.** In this activity, you want students to listen to a sequence of separately spoken phonemes and to then combine the phonemes to form a word. Students then write and read the word. For example, ask students, "What word is /d/ /o/ /g/? Students should sound each phoneme out and then blend the phonemes to say *dog.* Then ask students to write the sounds in *dog.* After they write the word, they should say the word aloud.

- *Identifying sounds in a story.* This activity allows students to integrate literature with phonemic awareness. Read a story with students. After you are finished reading the story, select a sound that appears throughout the story. Initially, you may want to choose a sound that appears at the beginning of words because this is the easiest. Then ask students to find this sound at the end of a word and even in the middle. You can go through the whole story identifying the chosen sound.

- *Identification of rhyming words.* This can be taught through the repetition of songs, poems, nursery rhymes, and chants. Choose an appropriate piece of text to repeat several times; usually, it is best if it is repeated several times initially and then revisited on a regular basis over time. Read the piece of text to students once. Ask them if they notice anything. Make sure to point out the rhyming at the end of the line. Read the passage a second time, but this time around, have students raise their hands every time they hear a rhyming word.

- *Inventing rhyming words.* Read a passage full of rhyming words to students several times. After students are familiar with a passage that has a recognizable rhyming pattern, cover up random rhyming words throughout the story and allow students to make up their own rhyming words that may fit into the text.

- *Find your match.* Give each student a card with a word written on it. Ask students to find the word that "matches" theirs. This can mean that students need to find the person who has a word that rhymes with theirs, has the same initial sound, or has the same ending sound. This can be repeated as many times as you can keep students' attention. For students who are still having difficulties reading, as many students will be at this stage, it may be more helpful to put a picture instead of a word on these cards.

- *Sound guessing.* In a bag, have simple objects that relate to the story being read to students. You may want to begin with objects that only have three sounds. This simplifies the process. Put your hand in the bag and grab an object. Give students clues as to what you are holding in your hand. Then pronounce the phonemes of the object you are holding. For example: "I have an object in my hand that you write with /p/ /e/ /n/." Make sure to emphasize the distinct phonemes. Have students repeat the phonemes to you and then blend the phonemes together. If students become very good at this, you may want to add more difficult words with more sounds.

- *Categorizing sounds.* Show students a set of three or four words. Once you have chosen the words, you need to make sure that one of the words has an "odd" sound. For example, ask students which of the following words doesn't belong: *hat, hot, rat.* Students should say that the word *rat* does not belong because it does not begin with /h/. You can do this with ending sounds as well.

Teaching Vocabulary

What It Is and What Research Can Tell Us

With respect to reading instruction, students' vocabulary is comprised of words that they know or recognize in their written form. Nagy and Herman (1987) estimate that the average students in grades 3 through 12 learn approximately 3,000 new words each year. Students' vocabulary has a direct bearing on reading comprehension in all texts and on their ability to communicate effectively both orally and in writing (National Institute of Child Health and Human Development, 2000). Students with large vocabularies are better readers and communicators than students with meager vocabularies.

Additionally, knowledge of word meanings is crucial for success in school and in life. Vocabulary development is an especially important area of focus when teaching poor, urban children. Moats (2001) reports on the significant gap in word knowledge between affluent and poor urban children, which he calls "word poverty." Garcia (1991) reports that many students for whom English is not their first language have difficulties understanding abstract English words (e.g., freedom) found in content textbooks.

We have four kinds of vocabularies: listening, speaking, reading, and writing. A child's first vocabulary is his or her listening vocabulary, but gradually, through school experiences, a child's reading vocabulary increases to become the largest of all of them.

Three major types of vocabulary words developed in elementary school reading programs are basic service, meaning, and content words. Basic service or sight words are the most common words in our language and make up a significant percentage of the words read each day. Many authors have developed lists of basic service or sight words, with the most popular one made by Edward Dolch (1948). Students need to learn basic service words "by sight"—that is, they need to recognize them instantly.

The second type of vocabulary words—meaning words—are words that are of interest to students at the various grade levels and those words that comprise students' literature and reading texts. The third type—content words—are specific to the various subject areas (e.g., math, social studies, and science). All three types of vocabulary words increase a student's reading comprehension and communication abilities.

Increasing children's vocabulary requires above all else the allocation of sufficient instructional time for both vocabulary instruction and meaningful, collaborative practice. Practice needs to include an abundance of oral discussions of new words, games and activities, and opportunities to use new words in contextual situations—that is, in actual sentences and stories (Apthorp, 2006).

Teacher Behaviors

- Assess students' mastery of basic sight vocabulary.
- Teach basic sight words through the whole word approach.
- Provide abundant repetition of new words.
- Focus on word learning throughout the day in all subject areas.
- Engage students in discussing new words (i.e., interactive talk).
- Relate new words and concepts to children's background experiences.

- Provide both direct/explicit instruction and implicit/indirect instruction in word learning.

- Provide students with a multitude of practice opportunities that actively engage them in applying new words to real reading situations.

Teaching Strategies

1. *The whole word approach for teaching basic service or sight words.* This approach to increasing vocabulary is a visual-auditory technique with little actual analysis of word parts. In the whole word approach (sometimes called the sight word approach), students learn a word by looking at it as a whole, not by dissecting it. The steps in the whole word approach are:

   a. Present individual words visually to students as you pronounce the words. It is important that students look at each word while you actually say the word.

   b. Discuss the meaning of the word, and use it in sentences.

   c. You and your students should pronounce the word over and over and use it in different sentences.

   d. Use a variety of games, computer programs, and teacher-made exercises to reinforce the new words in sentences and stories so that students will know them "by sight."

2. *Multisensory adaptation of the whole word approach for sight words.*

   a. Follow steps *a* and *b* in number 1.

   b. Using a cooking tin with fine, white sand, ask students to write the word in the sand as they slowly say the word.

   c. Smooth the sand and repeat step *b.*

   d. Ask students to write the new word on a sheet of paper.

   e. Write the word in a sentence, and have students read the sentence to you.

   f. Repeat steps *b* through *e* until students have mastered the word.

   g. Use a variety of games, computer programs, and teacher-made exercises to reinforce the new words in sentences and stories so that students will know them "by sight."

3. *Guided reading plan.* Teach new words in prereading (the "before reading" step), and review the words in the postreading ("after reading" step).

4. *Discuss with students* words that accompany stories being reading silently or orally.

5. *Allocate classroom time for wide/independent reading.*

6. *Teach the various context clues*—both semantic and syntactic—and discuss how meanings of words are determined.

7. *Directly teach synonyms and antonyms.*

8. *Directly teach word structure skills* or the elements of structural analysis: prefixes, suffixes, and the use of an affix in a syllabication strategy.

9. *Use semantic maps* to teach new words.

10. *Teach new words by the generative approach*—for example, teach Latin and Greek roots and the many English words that generate from each root.

11. *Teach new words from students' content-area textbooks.*

12. *Utilize various computer programs* to promote word learning.

13. *Practice, practice, practice.* Students need lots of practice in a variety of situations using a variety of materials to learn words. An abundance of easy reading on their independent level and the use of a variety of games and activities during shared reading, guided reading, paired reading, and small-group and individual work, as well as independent formats, such as learning stations, computer programs, and tape assisted reading, will enhance students' vocabulary. The more varied, interesting, and meaningful the practice afforded, the better are the chances for success.

Activities

- *Classroom labels.* Label objects in the classroom using short phrases, such as "the doors," "the wall," "a light switch," and so forth. Direct students' attention to these phrases on a regular basis. Make sure you place the labels at students' eye level.

- *Bingo.* Bingo-type games that require students to match a flashed word with the identical word on a bingo card can help students understand which features of the word are necessary to recognize it. You can pronounce the words and have students find the appropriate words on their bingo card.

- *"Felt" words.* Make sight words out of felt material or sandpaper. Have students practice tracing the word and saying it at the same time.

- *Cut-up sentences.* Design a series of sentences using previously studied sight words. Cut up the sentences into individual words and phrases. Have students, individually or in pairs, combine the parts into meaningful sentences and then read them aloud to you or other students. A variation is to design sight-word sentences and put them in a paper bag. Have students draw a sentence from the bag. If they can read the sentence, they can keep it.

- *Climb the ladder.* Design a poster-board ladder that has open slots at each step. Place sight words that have been studied during the week in the slots. Students are to "climb" to the top of the ladder by pronouncing each word and using it in a sentence. This exercise may be completed individually or with a partner. A variation is to design a baseball stadium and obtain miniature players. Have the student "at bat" look at a sight-word card. If he or she knows one word on sight, the "hit" is a single; two cards in a row make a "double," three a "triple," and four a "homer." Missing a word equals an "out."

- *Hanger words.* Have students write sight words on poster-board strips, and use string to hang the words on coat hangers. Hang the coat hangers from the ceiling or chalkboard. Periodically throughout the week, have students pronounce the words, write the words, and use them in a sentence. A variation is to have students arrange the words in meaningful sentences and phrases.

- *Pronoun referents.* Provide students with short, written phrases, such as: "It began to bark." "It is very green." "He took us to the game." Ask students to select from a list of choices those words that go with each phrase; for example, "The dog began to bark." "The grass is very green." "Father took us to the game."

- *Understanding relationships among words.* Give students several words that are related and ask them to identify others that are appropriate to the given words. The words supplied by students can be similar or opposite in meaning and should be based on their reading of stories and books.

  Similar meanings can include:
  > Big, huge, . . . (giant, grand, jumbo)
  > Small, tiny, . . . (minute, wee, miniature)
  Opposite meanings can include:
  > Big, huge, . . . (small, tiny, minute)
  > Shout, yell, . . . (whisper, soft, quiet)

Ask students to provide context and to write their context sentence for each of the words. After students understand the relationships between the words, have them provide additional words that retain similar meaning in the sentences.

- *Associating words with known concepts in context.* Keep an accurate list of new words that students encounter and learn. Words that contain the same root, prefix, or suffix and words in concept classifications can form the basis for expanding meaning vocabularies. Teach new words by relating them to similar words students already know. In interest areas, such as basketball, connect new words to the concept in a meaningful context. For example, connect *court, score, second, scoreboard, bounce, shot, shoot, dribble, foul, rebound, time-out,* and *rim.*

- *Using categories for classification of words.* Connect new words to words and concepts students already know for new word categories. For example, using the word *basketball,* illustrate word relationships with the same roots, prefixes, and suffixes. You can also classify words that students know from their reading of literature and basal stories in terms of similar properties, and introduce new words that relate to the known properties.

Teaching Phonics and Word Recognition

What It Is and What Research Can Tell Us

The ability to pronounce and interpret written symbols—to recognize unknown words—is an integral component of the reading process. Good readers are superior in this ability, while poor readers and beginning readers have trouble with it. However, identifying words is not reading but is a means for developing reading efficiency. Once students have learned ways to automatically decode words (i.e., to identify words quickly with minimal effort), they can devote most of their available attention to processing the text for meaning (Samuels, 1988).

The four major strategies used to recognize or decode unknown words are phonics, structural analysis, contextual analysis, and sight vocabulary. These four strategies together comprise a balanced word recognition program. They are taught concurrently in elementary school because one word recognition or decoding strategy will not be successful in all reading situations. Thus, readers need to develop a flexible, problem-solving approach to identifying unknown words (Durkin, 2004).

Phonics is a compilation of the connections or correspondences that exist between letters and the sounds they record in syllables used to help readers pronounce unknown words. In essence, phonics allows students to use the spelling of a word to get help with its pronunciation. Our language is an alphabetic one in that written words represent a collection of speech sounds, and this fact allows us to use phonics, a method to relate letters to the speech sounds that they represent. Reading programs must teach the content of phonics in the early grades in a direct/explicit fashion (National Institute of Child Health and Human Development, 2000). In addition, phonic instruction must include many opportunities for practice and transfer to new reading situations in everyday reading and writing activities (Armbruster, Lehr, & Osborn, 2001).

For youngsters trying to figure out words not yet in their reading vocabulary, it is an unfortunate reality that a lawful, one-to-one correspondence does not exist between sound and symbol. The English language has many more speech sounds than letters to represent them (26 letters, but anywhere from 42 to 46 speech sounds). Nevertheless, letter-sound generalizations and factors affecting letter-sound correspondences warrant the teaching of phonics to provide one way for students to identify unknown words on their own.

The second strategy for recognizing unknown words—structural analysis—focuses on meaningful structural units. In structural analysis, students identify a word's syllables, root element, prefixes, suffixes, compound elements, contractions, and inflectional endings to decode the word. As with phonics, the use of structural analysis depends on meaningful practice in context.

Contextual analysis is the third strategy for decoding unknown words and involves teaching students to use semantics (the meaning of other words in a sentence and paragraph) to arrive at the pronunciation and meaning of an unknown word, and syntax (the arrangement of word order) to determine the word's part of speech and whether it is singular or plural. Conscious use of context enables readers to arrive at the pronunciation and meaning of many words. Again, as is the case with the other word-decoding strategies, contextual analysis (using both semantic and syntactic clue systems) is rarely used by itself but is best combined with phonics or structural analysis in decoding unknown words.

The fourth and final strategy for recognizing unknown words involves sight vocabulary, which is comprised of the most common words in the English language (sometimes called basic service words), words of interest to students, words that appear regularly in students' first readers, and content-area words. Many sight words in the English language are irregular in nature (do not have a one-to-one sound/symbol relationship) and are taught using the whole-word or sight-word approach. In this approach, students learn a word by looking at it as a whole, not dissecting it (please see Chapter 9 for a complete description of this approach and practice activities). It is assumed that students will learn to identify these words by sight or instantly when presented with them. Words are presented visually to students, pronounced by both teacher and students, discussed and used in sentences, and practiced independently by students. In almost every instance, words learned through the whole-word or sight-word approach need to be practiced in context in a variety of ways.

Teacher Behaviors

- Specify clear instructional goals.

- Do not penalize students for dialectal errors in oral reading as long as reading comprehension is unaffected.

- Use the explicit/direct model of instruction to teach content with an abundance of meaningful practice.

- Monitor student progress.

- Foster a flexible, problem-solving approach in using phonics, structural analysis, contextual analysis, and sight words.

- Provide immediate feedback to students.

- Coach or assist students in the application of skill or strategy in real reading situations.

Teaching Strategies

1. *Analytic phonics.* Begin with a certain number of words that your students know, and have students examine the relationships between the phonic elements. Using the direct/explicit teaching approach, there are two basic ways of teaching a phonics lesson analytically:

   - Inductive—Give examples illustrating a generalization, and guide students to a conclusion.

   - Deductive—Tell students the generalization, and then ask them for examples to verify it.

     The following is an example of the inductive approach: Assume that students know the words *ball, bat,* and *bundle.* Ask students what is alike about the words. Students should discover that the words contain the letter *b,* which represents the /b/ sound. Ask students to tell you other words with the sound of /b/. Have students put the words into sentences and read the sentences aloud. Give students practice exercises for using the words in sentences.

The following is an example of the deductive approach: List the words *ball, bat,* and *bundle* on the chalkboard (assuming that the words are in students' listening-speaking vocabulary). Tell students that all the words begin with the letter *b* and represent the /*b*/ sound as in *big*. Ask students to tell you other words with the sound of /*b*/. Have students put the words into sentences and read the sentences aloud. Give students practice exercises for using the words in sentences.

2. *Synthetic phonics.* Begin immediately with instruction of individual phonics elements. Once students learn the sounds represented by the letters, they blend the parts of the words together to form a known word. In synthetic phonics, there are three variations of sound blending: (1) letter by letter (*b-a-t*); (2) the initial consonant is sounded, and the rest of the word is added as a word family (*b-at*); and (3) the initial consonant with the vowel is sounded together and then the final consonant (*ba-t*).

3. *Word families or phonograms.* Teach your students various clusters of sounds in words—sometimes called word families or phonograms. For example, a common phonogram is *ake,* as in the word *bake.* After teaching students the pronunciation of *ake,* guide them into substituting different beginning sounds with the same cluster of letters and pronounce words such as *rake, sake, take, lake, shake, make,* and *cake.* In this method, there is no need to isolate sounds as students learn to look for known letter clusters in new words. This method is also called "onsets and rimes" with the cluster of letters that rhyme called the "rime" and the preceding letter or letters called the "onset."

4. *Explicit/direct instruction for structural analysis and context.* In addition to teaching the content of phonics in a direct manner, teach the elements of structural analysis and the use of context clues to students in a step-by-step fashion, followed by both guided and independent practice opportunities.

Activities

* **Matching pictures and words.** Show students a picture of an object and follow it by four words, none of which names the picture but one or more of which begin with the same sound as the name of the pictured object. Ask students to draw a circle around the boxes or words that begin with the same sound. You can do this with final consonant sounds as well.

* **Identifying sounds in words.** Show students a series of boxes, each containing three words. Pronounce one of the words, and direct students to underline the word pronounced. Students need not know all of the words as sight words, provided they are familiar with the initial sound of each.

Example:

1	2	3	4	5
call	tell	hill	may	hat
bank	sell	fill	pay	show
play	fell	bill	say	bat

- *Matching words:* In columns, present words, some of which begin with the same sound and the same letter. Ask students to draw a line from the word in column A to the word in column B that begins with the same sound.

  Example:

A	B
me	be
ball	said
sail	make

- *The final sounds in candy.* Make a list of different names of candies. Begin with the first kind of candy on the list, say the name of the candy, and emphasize the final consonant students hear. Do this for all the candy on the list. You may want to put students into groups to brainstorm other words that end with the final sounds you have been working on. Record students' responses on the chalkboard.

- *Introducing initial consonants.* Print an uppercase letter on the board, and tell students they will learn all about that letter. Next to the uppercase letter, print the lowercase letter (example: Bb). Begin to write words that begin with lowercase *b.* Point to each word, and pronounce it by stressing the initial sound *b* without distorting it. Direct students to look at each word as it is pronounced, and ask if they can give any other words with the sound heard in the words. When a student gives the name of a person that starts with the letter *b,* tell students that we write that name with a capital *B* because it is somebody's name. Make sure you give lots of examples. Note that in no instance are students asked to sound the letter *b* in isolation.

- *Identifying objects.* Show students a picture of an object they will be able to recognize. Then show students a row of pictures, and ask them to mark the objects whose names begin with the same sound as the name of the object in the first picture shown. You can do this with final consonants as well.

- *Matching pictures and words.* Show students a picture of an object that is followed by four words, none of which names the picture but one or more of which begin with the same sound as the name of the pictured object. Ask students to draw a circle around the boxes or words that begin with the same sound. You can do this with final consonant sounds as well.

- *Vowel patterns.* Select a few easy words that have been used previously and that contain the vowel pattern being taught. Write these words in a column, and pronounce each word with students. Have students note the vowel letter in the middle of the word, and emphasize the sound it represents—for example, the *e* in *met, set,* and *pet.*

- *Single-double vowel patterns.* Prepare lists of words in which column A has a single vowel (e.g., *met*) and column B is identical except for an added vowel (e.g., *meat*). Ask students to read the first word under column A and to listen for the short vowel sound. Then ask them to read the first word under column B, to note the two-vowel pattern, and to listen for the long vowel sound. As a final step, have them read each pair in rapid succession to note the contrasting vowel sound (such as *met-meat* and *led-lead*).

- ***The effect of final* e.** On the chalkboard, write a column of words that contain the medial vowel *a*. As you pronounce these words, have students tell you which vowel sound they hear in the word *(a)*. Explain that you will change each word by adding the letter *e* at the end. Create a second column with the words from the first column, and add the letter *e*. As you pronounce these words, have students note the *a__e* pattern, and ask them to tell you the vowel sound they hear in each of the words. Be sure to mention that in many short words with two vowels, a final *e* is not sounded, while the first vowel has its long sound. Do many exercises with students, and have them say each word aloud.

- ***Long vowel sounds at the end of short words.*** Two generalizations cover single vowels at the end of words: (1) If a word has only one vowel that ends the word, the vowel sound usually is long, and (2) if a word has no other vowel and ends with *y*, the letter *y* serves as a vowel and is pronounced as long *i*. These generalizations apply in a limited number of high-frequency words and can be taught at the chalkboard, using columns of words. Utilize activities similar to those previously listed.

- ***Short-vowel packages.*** Create five packages, and label each package with a different vowel sound. Tape each package to a wall or chalkboard. Ask students to describe the packages and what is on the packages. Once students have noticed that all five packages contain a vowel, review all the sounds each *short* vowel makes. Ask students to give examples of words that contain the short vowel sound. Give each student five index cards. Instruct students to draw and label pictures of words containing the short vowel sound. You may want to do a few as a whole group so students know exactly what to do. Have students take turns reading their short-vowel picture cards and then taping them on the appropriate package.

- ***Prefix and suffix strips.*** After teaching particular prefixes and suffixes, put them on poster-board strips, and supply several root words as well. Ask students to make as many words as they can from the strips. As a final activity, ask students to put their new words into sentences.

- ***Syllable counting.*** Provide students with individual cards with the numbers 1, 2, 3, and 4 written on them. Pronounce various words with different numbers of syllables, and ask the students to raise the card indicating the number of syllables they hear in each word.

- ***Semantic clues.*** Provide students with sentences, leaving out one of the words. Ask the students to supply the correct word, and discuss the reasons why their word makes sense.

- ***Word order completion.*** Write sentences on the chalkboard, and leave out the verb (or noun, adjective, or adverb). Ask students to supply the appropriate word, and discuss why their choices are correct.

Developing Fluency

What It Is and What Research Can Tell Us

Fluency is the ability to pronounce or decode words quickly, smoothly, or automatically with expression, using little conscious effort and with comprehension. The ability to understand and react to ideas expressed in writing is the essence of reading. However, this is only possible if students can first decode words with ease—that is, if students can accurately and effortlessly pronounce and interpret written symbols. Simply put, successful readers are fluent readers, and struggling readers are not (Torgesen & Hudson, 2006). The key idea is that readers are not just good decoders but that they do it quickly. By being able to identify words automatically, readers have more time to think about and to react to the meaning of what they are reading (Rasinski and Padak, 2004). In other words, readers can devote almost total attention to the comprehension process. Without fluency, students must devote considerable time and effort to figuring out unfamiliar, individual words, and they simply cannot give their undivided attention to the meaning of the whole text.

Teacher Behaviors

- Explicitly or directly teach accuracy decoding or word identification skills and strategies to students.

- Provide interesting and varied practice in a number of contexts to students so that their decoding or word identification abilities become automatic.

Teaching Strategies

1. *Repeated readings.* This strategy requires students to reread a section of text several times until they achieve a high degree of fluency (Samuels, 1997). Repeated readings promote fluency and confidence, as many students never have had the opportunity to experience this feeling of effortless oral reading. Samuels provides steps for using this method:

   a. Select passages from 50 to 200 words long from stories students are reading.

   b. Read the passage to students, followed by students reading the passage several times until they can read the passage fluently (you may want to tape-record the first and last oral reading so students can hear the difference).

   c. Discuss with students how athletes develop their skills by practicing basic movements over and over until they become automatic and how repeated reading is similar in terms of practice.

   d. Have students time themselves reading a passage, and make a graph showing improvement in reading times.

2. *Phrase reading.* Phrase reading is another strategy for promoting students' fluency/automaticity. The basic steps in using this strategy are:

   a. Select reading material that is on the student's easy or independent level.

b. On a one-to-one basis, ask the student to read one paragraph or page aloud, and tape-record this reading.

c. Model for the student, reading the paragraph or page in a word-by-word fashion and in meaningful phrases.

d. Using a pencil (you may want to reproduce the text for ease of marking), divide the first two sentences into meaningful phrases. Another method is to reproduce the reading material by typing it in phrases in a vertical column.

e. Divide the rest of the sentences into meaningful phrases, with both you and the student contributing to how a sentence should be divided.

f. Have the student read the text aloud in meaningful phrases two or three times. You may want to read the phrases aloud together with the student.

g. Tape the last oral reading, and compare this tape with the tape of the initial reading of the text.

h. Discuss with the student the benefits of reading sentences in meaningful phrases as opposed to word-by word reading.

3. *Readers' theater.* This is a technique that allows students the opportunity to increase their fluency by practicing and reading aloud a scripted story (Sloyer, 1982). The steps are as follows:

a. Choose a narrative text on students' instructional or independent reading level.

b. Read and discuss the story with students.

c. Devise a script cooperatively with students and choose parts.

d. Have students practice their script by themselves and with their peers to promote fluency of oral reading.

e. Rehearse the script as a group.

f. Perform the play script in front of the class or small group.

g. Review the performance with students, noting how well the performance went and discussing the key ideas in the story.

4. *Paired reading.* Pair up students who have similar instructional levels and have them alternately read a few sentences aloud to one another. Repeat this process until students can read the sentences smoothly with expression. Any type of text is desirable for this technique. Don't forget to use practical or real-life materials, such as the Yellow Pages, store catalogs, the sports page from the local newspaper, and local community-center flyers.

Fostering Comprehension

What It Is and What Research Can Tell Us

Comprehension is the active, internal process of understanding ideas represented in text. Very simply, reading is comprehension. In essence, readers construct meaning from the ideas represented in the text based on their own prior knowledge and experiences. Thus, reading comprehension is the active process of "making sense" of what we read (Pearson, 2009).

The ultimate success of a reading program is the degree to which students can read and understand numerous texts for a variety of purposes. Success in comprehension is achieved through the coming together of a positive attitude, a rich background of knowledge and experiences, the explicit teaching and mastery of reading skills and strategies spanning different cognitive levels in both narrative and expository text, and the ability to monitor and regulate personal reading depending on the situation. Reading comprehension is best viewed as a multifaceted process affected by several thinking and language abilities. The ability to comprehend on different levels exemplifies the types of thinking that can be applied to written and oral language. The three different levels of thinking applied to reading comprehension are defined as follows:

- *Literal comprehension*—Understanding ideas and information explicitly stated in a passage

- *Inferential comprehension*—Understanding ideas and information implied in a passage

- *Critical comprehension*—Analyzing, evaluating, and personally and creatively reacting to information in a passage

To make sense of what they are reading and respond in a critical fashion, students must be shown how to be "strategic" in their reading. "Strategic" readers "think" about their reading before, during, and after reading a selection. They establish purposes for and monitor their reading, recognizing when to slow down, speed up, reread, or pause to understand a point. Knowing how one reads, coupled with the ability to "change gears" while reading, is called *metacognition*.

Central to the development of strategic readers is the important role of you, the classroom teacher. Only through your careful, expert planning, teaching, and guidance will students grow into mature, independent readers. Two major teaching strategies for fostering strategic reading abilities are *informing* and *modeling*. *Informing* involves explaining the new strategy in small steps, using examples and counterexamples. Informing further means telling students the "what," "when," and "why" of a strategy to help in understanding a generalization. *Modeling* involves demonstrating or showing students how to perform a particular strategy. Helping or assisting students to learn a new strategy is called "scaffolded instruction" (Rosenshine & Meister, 1995). Scaffolds are forms of support given to students in learning something new and the timely withdrawal of those supports as students demonstrate mastery. Examples of scaffolds or forms of support include modeling a strategy, giving students a sheet explaining how to summarize a story, and using a chart of the "reporter questions" *who, what, where, when, why,* and *how* to support the prereading strategy of predicting.

Teacher Behaviors

- Specify clear instructional goals.

- Explain, model, and scaffold reading comprehension skills and strategies.

- Design collaborative activities with students to discuss and analyze stories.

- Monitor student progress.

- Provide immediate feedback to students.

- Discuss application of skill or strategy in real reading situations.

Teaching Strategies

1. *Always establish purposes* for students before reading, and train students to set their own purposes.

2. *Use prereading strategies* (e.g., mental imagery, semantic maps, story maps, and other graphic organizers) to activate students' background knowledge, provide information for making predictions, show key relationships, and teach new vocabulary.

3. *Relate the text to be read to your students' background of experiences,* and show your students how to do this themselves, by asking appropriate questions using information from the text and visual aids.

4. *Explicitly explain the various types of text structures* (narrative and expository), and show students how to determine a text structure while they are reading.

5. *Teach students to use the reciprocal teaching approach* of Palinscar and Brown (1984), utilizing the four strategies of predicting, question asking, summarizing, and clarifying.

6. *On a regular basis, ask your students a variety of questions* requiring different levels of thinking. It is imperative to encourage them to think at various cognitive levels. Your art of questioning directly affects students' attitudes toward understanding text and, ultimately, how much they learn. In conjunction with asking a balanced set of questions that require different levels of thinking, practice the proven techniques of wait-time (also called think-time). This term denotes the period of silence after you ask questions but before students respond. Research has shown that if teachers wait three to five seconds before eliciting a response, students are better able to digest the question, and positive results occur (Rowe, 1974). More student participation, linger responses, and more high-level thinking are among the positive effects of this technique. In addition to wait-time, you need to be equipped with "probing questions" to help redirect or expand students' responses to a question. To keep discussions lively and extend students' thinking, ask thought-provoking questions,

such as "Can you tell me more?" What are some other ideas?" and "Do you agree or disagree with the author?"

7. *Teach students the Question-Answer Relationships (QAR) strategy* (Raphael, 1982). In this strategy, students learn to identify the source of information required in answering comprehension questions. The four sources of information or relationships between a question, the text, and the reader's own background knowledge are:

   a. *Right there*—The answer to a question can be found right there in the text.

   b. *Think and search*—The answer requires the student to search the text for information and to think about various pieces of information to arrive at the answer.

   c. *Author and you*—The answer requires both information from the text and the reader's background of experiences.

   d. *On my own*—The answer to a question is not in the text but lies within the reader's background.

8. *Directly explain, model, or demonstrate specific comprehension skills and abilities* to students, and practice an abundance of interesting and varied drills for the skill or ability to become automatic. The direct or explicit instruction method—a universal teaching strategy that has been used for years—has as the heart of the lesson the systematic explanation, demonstration, or modeling of the new skill or ability. The basic steps in this approach are readiness, step-by-step explanation of the lesson objective, guided practice, and independent practice.

9. *Using an actual student text, model for students exactly how and why* they should slow down, speed up, stop, use a visual aid (to better understand the ideas expressed in the text), pause to make note of an important point, reread a section (to understand an ideas), and answer end-of-chapter questions.

10. *Teach students the meanings of the "reporter questions"*—who, what, where, when, why, and how. Practice finding the answers to various "reporter questions" in a story or chapter. Model for students how you would ask yourself "reporter questions" while reading and how you would quiz yourself after reading using the same questions.

Activities

- ***Picture details.*** Provide students with a short story or passage appropriate to their abilities and experiential backgrounds. Represent the major story details with pictures placed on separate cards. The pictures can represent major events, characters, settings, and so forth. For example, if in the story the main characters went to a lake to go fishing, set up a tent, wore warm clothing, and cooked their food over a campfire, then each detail can be represented on separate picture cards. Provide students with the cards appropriate to their story. Instruct them to select cards representing the details of the story they read, which are turned over to you after they complete the activity. A variation is to either record stories on audiotape or use read-along stories. Have students listen to the story and then select story details from picture cards.

- *Finish the story.* Provide students with a short story or several connected paragraphs to read. On a separate sheet of paper, provide incomplete information about the story's content. For example: "This story is about Joe, who wanted to _____. Joe's mother did not agree with Joe's choice because _____." Direct students to read the incomplete sentences first and then to read the story to fill in the missing information. Make sure students understand that more than one word is required to fill in the information that is missing.

- *You decide.* Give students two short stories or connected paragraphs. Tell them to read the text and then to decide if information listed on separate story cards belongs to either reading selection, and if so, which one. Students can read an event card aloud, and other students can respond about which story contained the event, character, setting, etc. Students who respond correctly get to keep the story card.

- *A thousand words.* Provide students with a short story or several related sentences to read. Direct them to draw a picture that best represents the main idea of the story. A variation is to have them draw a series of pictures in cartoon fashion that represents literal information found in their reading.

- *Character.* Prepare several short descriptions of different characters. Have students read the descriptions and categorize the characters in terms of their descriptions. A variation would be to give students a visual format, such as a flowchart or wheel and spokes, and have them fill in each part with the descriptive words.

- *Does it make sense?* Cut apart stories and paste the pieces on separate pieces of cardboard. Have students arrange the stories in a manner that makes sense. A variation of this is to have students arrange all but a part of the story in a manner that makes sense. Have students read each other's stories to see if they can find the part that does not make sense. A variation is to have students experiment with the stories to see if they can be combined or organized in several ways and still make sense.

- *Headlines.* Prepare newspaper headlines appropriate to students' reading abilities and experiential backgrounds. Provide students with a headline, and direct them to compose a story appropriate to it. Before writing their stories, students should write out what would be necessary to help them in composing their stories. Use "reporter questions" to assist students in planning their stories. For example, with a headline such as "12-YEAR-OLD BOY CATCHES RECORD-SIZED FISH," students could possibly list information for "who" (name of the boy), "where" he lives, "why" he likes to fish, "where" he caught the fish, "when" he caught the fish, and how he felt when he caught it. Once students have listed the information related to the "reporter questions," have them write their stories. This activity helps students use their experiential background to construct meaning as they read and write stories.

- *Continuations.* Prepare a series of sentences such as, "Joe earned four dollars raking leaves for his mother." Prepare an equal number of sentences that are logical continuations for each of the other sentences. For example, a logical continuation for the previous sentence could be: "He spent three dollars to go to the afternoon movie." Have students read each sentence and then select a sentence that would be a logical continuation. A variation is to have students write their own sentences that would be logical continuations of the given sentences.

- *Finish the story.* Select a connected story, and delete every other sentence from it. Students can either write their own sentences that make sense for the ones that were deleted, or they can select from those that you provide.

  Example:
  "Mary was looking forward to going to the lake with her parents." "Mary spent two weeks at the same lake last summer and made several new friends."

- *Who buys it.* Provide students with a department store catalog and list of items found in the catalog. Direct students to read the description of each item and to infer the type of person or character traits of a person who might purchase such items. A variation of this activity involves using pictures of items in the catalog.

- *What I know.* Provide students with a brief overview of a story and pictures appropriate to the story. Before reading the story, have students list what they know about it. Direct students to read the story to confirm or reject the information they listed.

- *Questions to answer.* Provide students with brief information about a story before they are to read it. Such information could focus on the plot, characters, setting, etc. Then ask students to write a list of questions they would like to have answered as a result of reading the story. Students can write their answers to their own questions after they read the story.

- *Road map.* Give students a written map of a story they are to read (the map would highlight major story information). As students read, they are to predict what comes next in terms of alternate routes on the road map. Students test their predictions as they read the story and complete their map.

- *Who comes to the party.* Give students short descriptions about different characters, and then tell them that one of the characters is having a party and needs help making a guest list. Direct students to help complete a guest list by selecting people to come to the party. Students should write a brief paragraph or two about why they chose the particular characters they did.

Developing Critical Thinking

What It Is and What Research Can Tell Us

Harris and Hodges (1995) define critical thinking as "the thought processes characteristic of creativity and criticism in literature and other arts; divergent thinking." (p. 50). In most instances, there are no right or wrong answers in thinking critically or divergently about the ideas in text (as compared to convergent thinking, where there is always a "correct" answer). Critical-thinking abilities in reading instruction allow individuals to analyze, evaluate, and personally and creatively react to information presented in a text passage based on their own prior knowledge and past experiences.

With the shift to viewing reading as an active, creative, strategic, and problem-solving process, the topic of critical-thinking abilities as a goal in reading instruction has received renewed attention. In today's world, literacy involves much more than merely comprehending ideas on a literal or factual level. It involves the ability to thoughtfully assess, analyze, react to, and evaluate ideas and arguments. Specific examples of critical-thinking abilities are hypothesizing, summarizing, inferring, judging, looking for assumptions, and imagining. The critical reader is a reflective thinker, who responds with healthy skepticism to the text and in effect asks, "So what?"

Critical thinking doesn't develop by chance. If students are not instructed in thinking critically, they simply will not do so.

Teacher Behaviors

- Allocate sufficient instructional time for developing critical thinking.

- Explain, model, and demonstrate critical-thinking strategies to students.

- Scaffold or aid students in the application of a critical-thinking strategy.

- Monitor student progress.

- Be a critical reader yourself, and share this excitement with your students.

Teaching Strategies

1. *After reading a story, ask questions to tap higher-level thinking abilities.* While it is certainly easier to ask lower-level cognitive questions during story discussions, it is much more exciting and beneficial to students if they are routinely asked high-level questions. You should strive for a balance between low- and high-level questions during discussion periods.

2. *Directly or explicitly explain and model specific critical-thinking abilities,* such as summarizing and hypothesizing. Follow up with cooperative assignments that allow you to scaffold a particular critical-thinking ability with your students.

3. *Devise thinking assignments* for which students can apply their reading abilities. In such activities, students collect, organize, and criticize information on a topic of interest to them. In doing so, they must classify, interpret, and react critically to the information they read. A complete listing of thinking activities for all grade levels is found in the excellent book *Teaching for Thinking: Theory, Strategies,*

and Activities for the Classroom by Raths et al. (1986). Sample topics of creative assignments, which may be done individually or as group projects, include how humans study the weather; music of the 1970s; the lives and accomplishments of prominent Americans, such as Rosa Parks, General Colin Powell, Martin Luther King, Jr., former Interior Secretary Manuel Lujan, and President John F. Kennedy; oil and the Middle East; China today; and life in our city 50 years ago.

4. *When conducting a discussion with students, situations will develop in which the students must be redirected or put back on the right track.* They may need a question rephrased, or further elaboration, or they may need to be challenged to think critically. In such cases, give feedback with clarifying or probing questions. Clarifying questions are used to redirect and refine students' responses to a question. The following are examples of probing questions: "Are you sure you mean what you said?" "Can you give me another example?" "What are some other alternatives?" "Can you tell me more?" "What assumptions are you making?" "Can you explain why?" "Do you agree? Disagree? Why?"

5. *Use good literature,* including multicultural books, with your students. Gentile and McMillan (1989) recommend placing a greater emphasis on literature to promote higher-order thinking, especially with "at-risk" students. Their compelling rationale for using fine literary material is as follows:

> Literature is the vehicle for helping "at-risk" students make sense out of and through written language. It provides them the means to apply skills contextually, using rich material that educates and entertains. Moreover, good literature is knowledge-based and furnishes these students a broad range of historical, geographical, political, scientific, mathematical, religious, biological, and literacy information. It stirs wonderment and imagination, facilitates these students' understanding of themselves and others and the world they live in, and offers them a sense of identity or control that can empower the spirit and motivate them to express their thoughts and feelings. (p. 12)

Teaching a Story:
Guided Reading

What It Is and What Research Can Tell Us

Teaching a story is the road map teachers follow when reading a story with children. The centerpiece of teaching reading in American classrooms is a *story* (or some form of text, be it a content chapter, newspaper, or magazine article). Students are not told to open up to a story and begin reading. Instead, teachers point the way for students in reading a story by guiding them through specific steps to enhance reading comprehension (Heilman, Blair, & Rupley, 2002).

Whether the focus is on teaching vocabulary, decoding skills and strategies, comprehension skills and strategies, or content studying strategies, teachers use some type of story or text to help students to advance in their reading abilities. The "proof" of whether or not students have learned, and as a means to mark their improvement, is students' ability to actually apply new skills and strategies in a real story or some form of text.

Teachers use two major strategies to teach a story: shared reading (used primarily in beginning reading) and guided reading (used at all levels). Whether teaching a literature story, a story from a published reading series, a magazine article, or a content chapter in social studies or science, successful teachers use and adapt a reading game plan or scheme in teaching.

Teacher Behaviors

- Select stories on students' instructional level.

- Relate the stories to the lives and interests of students.

- Order activities so students will be on-task.

- Follow an instructional plan, such as shared reading or the Guided Reading Plan (see the section "Teaching Strategies," which follows), to teach a story.

- Help students see the relationship of the story to a larger whole.

- Assess students' understanding of the story content.

- Help students react creatively to the story.

Teaching Strategies

1. *Shared reading.* Use this popular procedure, which involves reading a book together with your students, primarily with beginning readers. During shared reading, teach several important understandings, such as word awareness (e.g., sentences are made up of words, and words are made up of letters), print awareness (e.g., top-down and left-to-right features of the English language, punctuation marks, and the concept of a title), and phonological awareness (e.g., phoneme segmentation and syllable counting). In addition, model what a story is and what expert readers say and do when reading. Usually, you read the stories aloud several times to students and initiate much conversation about the story. The flexible steps in the shared book experience are:

    a. Choosing a book based on students' interests and/or ability

b. Introducing the book, discussing the pictures, and having students predict the story line

c. Reading the book aloud to students and talking about the illustrations

d. You and the students rereading the book aloud together and talking about the story

e. Rereading the book to develop fluency and vocabulary development (this can be accomplished in small groups or pairs)

f. Completing an art, music, science, or social studies activity related to the story

2. *Guided Reading Plan.*

Before reading:

• Discuss prior knowledge and past experiences related to the story.

• Develop background information needed for reading the story.

• Develop interest in the story and motivation to read by relating the story to students' own lives. When possible, bring in real objects related to the story, play a record, show a short video, and so forth.

• Preteach new vocabulary in the story or text to be read.

• Preteach any new word identification or comprehension skill/strategy that your students will need to be successful in reading the story or text. Explain the new skill/strategy, and provide guided and independent practice on the targeted objective.

• Encourage students to ask purpose-setting questions about what will happen in the story and ask them to make predictions.

During reading:

• Remind students to answer any questions or predictions while they read silently and to make up new questions and predictions to guide their reading.

• Remind students to stop and reread difficult parts of the story.

• Remind students to ask for help if needed.

After reading:

• Answer purpose-setting questions, and discuss outcomes of predictions made before reading.

• Ask students comprehension questions about the story, and also have students ask their classmates comprehension questions about the story. When possible, design literature response groups, and have students respond to the story through discussion and/or writing.

• Clarify any ambiguous understandings by going back to the story and rereading parts aloud.

• Together with students, summarize the story.

• Review with students any new word identification and/or comprehension skill or strategy taught in the "before reading" section.

- Practice the new skills and strategies in a variety of groupings.

- Combine reading and writing on topics related to the story.

- Complete multidisciplinary activities (integrating skills and strategies in math, science, and social studies), language arts activities (grammar, spelling, and writing), and creative activities (panel discussions; word study; reading other books by the author; drama, music and art projects; and so forth) related to the story.

Developing Understanding in Content Reading

What It Is and What Research Can Tell Us

Content reading is the ability to comprehend ideas read in various subject area texts. We have known for years that success in the regular reading program does not automatically spell success in reading for content (Husbands & Shores, 1950).

While many of the skills and strategies developed in the regular reading program naturally carry over into content reading, these two types of reading differ significantly. Most of the stories students read during reading instruction are written in narrative form (with characters, setting, and plot), whereas content material is written in an expository structure (various patterns or styles, including sequential order, problem and solution, cause and effect, comparison and contrast, and descriptive). Expository text is usually at a higher readability or difficulty level because of the large number of concepts presented, and difficult vocabulary is presented in a different organizational pattern. Expository text is also characterized by its compact presentation of information. Students need to acquire specific skills and strategies to comprehend and construct meaning from their science, social studies, mathematics, and other technical texts.

Success in understanding any new content also requires students to learn and use specific studying and metacognitive strategies—before, during, and after reading content material (Paris, Lipson, and Wixon, 1994). Metacognition in reading is the reader's ability to be aware of and control his or her reading behavior. Without specific instruction in metacognitive strategies and specific guidance in reading content chapters, students experience great difficulty in learning. Viewing reading as a problem-solving activity, teachers should use a procedure similar to the Guided Reading Plan presented in Chapter 14 for teaching a story when using a content reading textbook chapter.

Teacher Behaviors

- Assess students' abilities to read content material.

- Apply a teaching strategy to guide students' comprehension in content chapters.

- Teach specific content skills and strategies needed for successful comprehension in students' science, social studies, mathematics, and other technical texts.

- Teach expository text patterns so students will better understand content material.

- Monitor students' understanding of content material.

Teaching Strategies

1. *Content Reading Guided Reading Plan.*

   Before reading:
   - Discuss prior knowledge and past experiences related to the chapter.
   - Develop background information needed for reading the new chapter.
   - Preteach new vocabulary.

- Preteach any specific skill/strategy related to the chapter, such as reading maps, tables, time lines, and graphs; outlining main ideas; classifying details and main ideas; using reference materials; or understanding a particular expository text structure.

- Ask students to read the introduction or first few paragraphs and discuss it.

- Examine all the visual aids throughout the chapter—pictures, maps, graphs, diagrams, and so forth, and discuss them with students.

- Ask students to read the chapter summary, and discuss it together.

- Ask students to read any questions at the end of the chapter and to answer any questions that can already be answered.

- Ask students to make predictions about the chapter content.

During reading:

- Ask students to turn each statement printed in bold into a question and read to find the answer.

- Remind students to use various fix-up or checking strategies, such as rereading to understand a point, summarizing a difficult idea, making notes in margins, hypothesizing about what will happen next, testing themselves about the meaning of key vocabulary and main ideas, highlighting main points in the text, and answering some of their predictions.

After reading:

- Discuss the chapter with students by asking them to answer their initial predictions or purpose-setting questions, as well as any end-of-chapter questions.

- Assist students in summarizing the chapter.

- Encourage students to reread parts of the chapter for clarification.

- Review with students any new comprehension skill or strategy taught in the "before reading" section.

- Practice new skills and strategies in a variety of groupings.

- Integrate the fine arts, such as music or art, into the ideas expressed in the chapter.

- Design extended activities related to the chapter, such as research projects, experiments, interviews, writing, and Internet searches.

2. *Reciprocal teaching.* Reciprocal teaching is another technique to teach a content chapter and is designed to improve students' comprehension abilities (Palinscar & Brown, 1984). The technique requires that you model comprehension strategies, followed by students themselves taking over the teaching role. Reciprocal teaching involves four comprehension tasks:

   a. Predicting

   b. Developing and answering questions

   c. Summarizing

   d. Clarifying difficult parts

Model each of the four comprehension tasks to students in reading a content chapter: Predict what a chapter will be about, and ask students to read the chapter silently. Next, ask questions about the chapter and answer them for students. Then summarize the chapter for students, and finally, clarify a difficult part for students by going back into the chapter and rereading a portion of text. With each successive chapter, have students gradually assume responsibility for each of the four tasks. You assume the student role but also monitor students' performance and provide needed feedback and encouragement.

3. *K-W-L.* A third teaching strategy to help students read content chapters is K-W-L. This strategy is designed to capitalize on students' knowledge of a topic before reading and to promote more active reading of expository text (Ogle, 1986). As discussed briefly in Chapter 3, the letters *K, W,* and *L* stand for three instructional steps: (1) students assess what they already *know,* (2) determine what they *want* to know, and (3) check what they *learned* from the reading. Students use a worksheet to record their responses to the three areas as the lesson progresses. In the first step, *K,* brainstorm with students about what they already know about the chapter. Then help students group what they know into categories. In the second step, *W,* guide students to generate questions they would like answered in their reading. In the last step, *L,* students write down what they learned from reading the content chapter. An example of a K-W-L worksheet concerning a chapter on Thailand is shown in Table 15-1.

4. *Explicit/direct instruction of specific content skills and strategies.* Specific reading skills and strategies are needed for the effective reading of particular content areas. Students' abilities in these areas need to be assessed and taught using the explicit/direct approach described in Appendix B. This instruction can be delivered separately in a content class or reading class, or can accompany the "after reading" section of the Content Reading Guided Reading Plan. The specific skills and strategies (among others) required for each of the following subjects include:

    Math—The abilities to (a) use a slow and deliberate reading rate, (b) master technical vocabulary and symbols, (c) follow directions, and (d) apply learned concepts in new situations.

    Social studies—The abilities to (a) follow ideas and events in sequences; (b) read maps, tables, time lines, and graphs; (c) outline main ideas; (d) follow directions; and (e) master specialized vocabulary.

    Science—The abilities to (a) follow sequence, (b) follow directions, (c) classify details and main ideas, (d) interpret graphic material visually, (e) apply learned concepts in new situations, and (f) master specialized vocabulary.

Table 15-1 Example K-W-L Worksheet Concerning a Chapter on Thailand

Thailand

K *(Know)*	W *(Want to Know)*	L *(Learned)*
Thailand is a country in Asia.	What are its principal cities?	Bangkok is the capital, and Chang Mai is a major city in the north.
It is near Vietnam.	What is the main religion of the Thai people?	Buddhism is the primary religion.
Tiger Woods is part Thai.	What goods does Thailand produce?	Silk, cotton, furniture, and jewelry are some of the goods produced in Thailand.
The country has beautiful temples.	What is the primary language in Thailand?	Thai is the main language.
	What is there to see in Thailand?	Ancient cities, temples, mountains, beaches, and museums are some of the sights of Thailand.
		Phuket is an island in Thailand where Tiger Woods played golf.

Categories of Information

Major cities_____

Primary religion _____

Goods and materials _____

Places to see _____

Common Core State Standards Based Reading Instruction

—*Sarah Adams Morton*

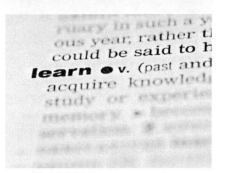

What It Is and What Research Can Tell Us

The Common Core State Standards (CCSS) are college and career ready student learning outcomes. The standards were created after an intensive national data analysis concluded that a majority of students graduating high school did not have the skill sets needed to be successful in college or in workforce training programs. The CCSS were developed using a backwards design—beginning with skills that are essential in college and career training and distilling those down through every single grade. The standards define what students need to learn but not how to teach them; teachers will continue to develop lessons and refine instruction based on the needs of their students. Currently adopted in 45 states, the CCSS create a common educational language and are internationally benchmarked targeting students success in a global economy and society.

The standards:

- Are aligned with college and work expectations;

- Are clear, understandable and consistent;

- Include rigorous content and application of knowledge through high-order skills;

- Build upon strengths and lessons of current state standards;

- Are informed by other top performing countries, so that all students are prepared to succeed in our global economy and society; and

- Are evidence-based (NGA Center and CCSSO, 2010).

Reading as a subject matter is part of the English Language Arts (ELA) section of the CCSS—also known as English Language Arts and Literacy in History/Social Studies, Science, and Technical Subjects. The ELA Standards are organized into three main sections: a comprehensive K–5 section; and two content-area–specific sections for grades 6–12, one for ELA and one for history/social studies, science, and technical subjects. One premise of Common Core implementation is that *all* teachers *are reading teachers* and all are required to support students with deep comprehension of complex texts. The reading standards call attention to text complexity and the growth of comprehension, placing equal emphasis on what students read and the skill with which they read.

In Reading, there are ten anchor standards that include essential reading skills. You can think of an anchor standard as an anchor keeping our students from floating away at anytime during their K–12 education. Each anchor standard is developed further through grade level progressions for reading literature and informational text. Additionally, students in grades K–5 are expected to master foundational skills, named appropriately *Reading: Foundation Skills,* which include concepts of print, the alphabetic principle, and other basic conventions of the English writing system.

Anchor standard 10 defines a grade-by-grade "staircase" of increasing text complexity that rises from beginning reading to the college and career readiness level (NGA Center and CCSSO, 2010).Text complexity considers qualitative, quantitative, as well as reader and task considerations. Qualitative evaluation of the text includes levels of meaning, structure, language conventionality and clarity, and knowledge demands. Quantitative measures can be calculated by computer programs and include readability measures. Variables specific to individual readers (such as motivation, knowledge, and experiences) and to tasks (such as purpose and the complexity of the task assigned and the questions posed) must also be considered when determining whether a text is appropriate for a given student. Students, especially striving students, need books written at their current reading levels to practice and build confidence. They also need to have regular interactions with more difficult, "complex" texts that challenge and push them forward. Just as it is impossible to build muscles without weight resistance, it's impossible to build robust reading skills without reading challenging text" (Shanahan, Fisher, & Frey, 2012).

Close, analytic reading stresses engaging students in examining text of sufficient complexity through deliberate reading and rereading. Reading and writing must also be grounded in evidence from text with students using the text first for responses in conversations and in writing about what they read. Directing student attention on the text itself empowers students to understand the central ideas and key supporting details . . . and ultimately leads students to arrive at an understanding of the text as a whole" (PARCC, 2011). Content-rich informational texts are highlighted as most required reading in college and workforce training programs is informational in structure and challenging in content. According to the standards, half of what elementary students read must be information. By 12th grade 70 percent of required reading must be informational texts. Instruction in academic vocabulary then becomes critical—this vocabulary is made up of mostly abstract words that appear in a wide variety of texts. These words are rarely well defined by context clues and are frequently encountered in complex text.

Teacher Behaviors

- Use student data and the CCSS as the basis of every lesson.

- Select increasingly complex text to build skill and stamina. Be familiar with the text you are teaching from.

- Integrate informational and content area literacy.

- Model close reading of all texts and include text dependent questions. Text dependent questions require specific reference to text and promoting deeper thought about the topic being addressed.

- Model questioning for students.

- Focus on academic vocabulary.

- Incorporate student discussion and written response to reading in all reading lessons.

- Create challenging lessons that gradually release responsibility and increase student independence.

- Provide time each day for independent reading of texts—at least 30 minutes.

- Integrate media and technology into all lesson sequences.

Teaching Strategies

1. Focus on comprehension from day one. Even beginning readers are capable of making sense of read-alouds.

2. Start with shorter passages. Use of short texts proves to be a promising practice for teaching students to read closely. Try short stories, articles, and poetry to begin. As students become more familiar with close reading, increase the amount of text used for this purpose.

3. Use student interests when choosing complex texts. Many students have natural interests in content area information which are by nature complex. Use information from student interest inventories to select challenging texts that your students want to read.

4. Don't give too much upfront (known as front-loading). Allow students to draw conclusions and make inferences through close reading of text. Make sure to not provide information that the student can learn through reading—this undermines reading as a learning tool.

5. Use directed text coding as a method to promote text-based evidence discussion and writing. When guiding students to read closely, give them a tool for marking the text for a specific reason.

6. Teach questioning directly. Students do not automatically know how to ask and answer questions. Create an anchor chart of question words (who, what, why, could, etc.) with students and post as a visual reference. Model question generation while reading. Importantly, respond to student's questions.

7. Use Pair-Share to encourage active writing and discussion. After posing a text based question, have students draft a written response. After adequate time has been given to write an initial response, have students pair up and choose one response to revise. Give students time to revise and then share with the rest of the class.

8. Base vocabulary lessons on words that will directly impact the student's level of understanding. The common core discourages use of prefab vocabulary lists and demand students learn strategies for learning new vocabulary words. Once you have selected key words, decide whether the text gives enough information to teach a strategy. If it does not, provide a simple definition to the students.

9. Directly teach word structure and context as the means to figuring out unknown vocabulary words. As you model reading aloud, stop at a challenging word and model both of these methods as a means to derive meaning. Let the students figure out the word using these strategies as soon as possible.

10. Provide daily opportunities for independent reading and writing. Nothing is better for reading and writing than reading and writing. Set aside time each day for students to read self-selected appropriate texts. It is important for you to model this behavior during this time.

11. Emphasize reading stamina. Reading complex text requires stamina from your readers. Encourage students to track their independent reading outside of school using incentive based rewards.

12. Practice "Close" Reading. In general, close reading requires multiple readings of complex texts—reading each time to find specific information. After at least two to three readings for specific purposes, students return to the text and read independently for an additional purpose. Close reading requires students to glean new information and often eliminates the need for students to pre-read the text. Pre-reading strategies are only used in cases where students cannot determine the learning goal from closely reading text. *See the lesson planning model exemplar below.*

Close Reading Lesson Planning Model Exemplar

To read closely, readers must interact repeatedly with text for specific purposes. The following provides guidelines for planning a close reading lesson.

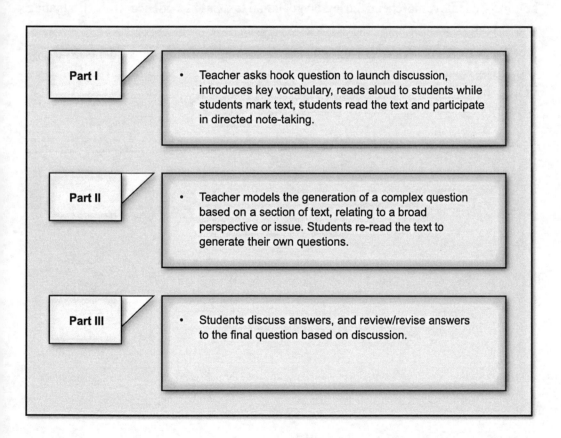

Part I
- Teacher asks hook question to launch discussion, introduces key vocabulary, reads aloud to students while students mark text, students read the text and participate in directed note-taking.

Part II
- Teacher models the generation of a complex question based on a section of text, relating to a broad perspective or issue. Students re-read the text to generate their own questions.

Part III
- Students discuss answers, and review/revise answers to the final question based on discussion.

BEGIN WITH DATA AND THE STANDARDS   When designing a Common Core reading lesson begin with a data analysis of your students and look across grade levels to determine gaps in the ELA standards for Literacy and Informational Text.

TEXT SELECTION   must be appropriate in content and adequately complex for the students intended, lend itself to opposing views and deep discussion, allow for cross-curricular discussion and encourage students to think more globally.

VOCABULARY   Vocabulary lessons are not required. When context clues or word structure assist with meaning, share that briefly with the students. Include general academic vocabulary as well as content-specific words in your preview of the text.

CODING (TEXT MARKING) AND NOTE TAKING   Use the text structure and content to create categories for coding and note-taking. Always try to code and mark yourself first to make sure your categories work with that text.

CREATING THE "HOOK" QUESTION   Make the question broad enough so that all students will be able to contribute. The question should activate prior knowledge that will help students better understand the concepts for the lesson.

WRITTEN RESPONSE   Throughout a close reading lesson, students actively engage in short response writing. The first written response can be built upon the hook question and the same as the second question, if you write "according to the text" before your second question. The final written response is more specific, asking students to cite textual evidence. All written response questions are tied to standard and are developed at the same time.

TEXT BASED DISCUSSION THROUGHOUT   Questions should stay focused on helping students comprehend the lesson goals and text based evidence while stimulating discussion.

STUDENT QUESTION GENERATION   Start by modeling for students. You may want to let students experiment at first with open questions. Questions can be developed before, during, and after reading and can be discussed either before or after the final writing.

Technology for the Reading Program

—Lourdes H. Smith

What It Is and What Research Can Tell Us

When considering the instructional goals and types of implementation required for a quality reading program, educators must also reflect on the use of technology in their everyday instruction. Technology use comes in many shapes and sizes while encompassing a variety of formats that provide opportunities to support learners in their literacy development. Over time this has been done via computer programs and games along with word processing utilities. In more recent times the Internet and other forms of information and communication technologies (ICTs), as deemed by the International Reading Association (IRA), are redefining the concept of literacy and will continue to do so as new forms of technology are created (IRA, 2009). Teachers must consider the transactional relationship between technology and literacy and how technology transforms the forms and functions of literacy while literacy transforms the forms and functions of technology (Leu, Kinzer, Coiro, & Cammack, 2004). Not only is technology being used as a part of our daily reading instruction to support our learners with reading, it is also responsible for the creation of new literacies that educators must acknowledge when working with the current and future curriculum.

Technology and its use is present in many areas of our lives and this is no different for our students. ICTs such as search engines, online games, websites, e-mail, Twitter, Facebook, mobile applications, instant messaging (IM), blogs, e-books, wikis, and YouTube are just a few of the numerous technologies available and that have led to the need for new literacies. In order to use and integrate these new literacies into instruction we must understand that the definition of literacy is constantly changing due to the new technologies used for communication and information (Leu, et al. 2004). Although there is no precise definition of the new literacies, they are often described as being multiple, multi-modal, and multifaceted, and offer educators new ideas when it comes to how to use technology in the reading classroom (Coiro, Knobel, Lankshear, & Leu, 2008). Youth engagement with online digital literacies and technologies are rapidly growing and there is concern regarding students having a more engaged life online and a less engaged life offline (Leu & Forzani, 2012). Teachers must work toward integrating literacy and technology-based instruction, with a focus on academic literacies, into their planning to ensure students are able to meet the needs of the 21st Century.

While keeping in mind those 21st Century critical literacies, we must, first and foremost, consider the needs of our students. As literacy educators we have the responsibility to prepare students for their present needs and the future goals. The IRA recognizes this and notes that students have the right to teachers who are skillful in using ICTs and embedding critical and cultural thinking into instruction, to peers that use ICTs responsibly, to a literacy curriculum that offers opportunities to worldwide collaboration with peers, to have access to ICTs, and to standards and assessments that include new literacies (2009). It is within the standards and assessments that new literacies and new technology are gaining much support.

The adoption and implementation of the Common Core State Standards (CCSS) are helping teachers respond to the need of integrating technology into everyday literacy lessons. One of the key design considerations for the CCSS describe a student who is college and career ready in reading, writing, speaking, and language as one that can "use technology and digital media strategically and capably" (National Governors Association Center for Best Practices & Council of Chief State School Officers [NGA, CCSSO], 2012). Starting in the primary grades, students are asked to use and explore digital tools and other types of media in order to meet the goals of the CCSS. Included are standards for students to use technology, including the Internet, to produce and publish writing while interacting and collaborating with other classmates (NGA, CCSSO, 2012). Intermediate students are asked to create and evaluate while using digital texts, digital sources, and other multimedia. The CCSS recognizes and supports the need for students to gain experiences with new technologies and new literacies from the beginning to end of their K–12 education.

Teacher Behaviors

As noted by the IRA (2009), teachers need to:

- Explore instructional models for using technology as part of literacy instruction.

- Participate in professional development on how to effectively use technology and literacy together.

- Provide thoughtful opportunities for technology use based on current research.

- Create specific lessons and assignments integrating both literacy and technology.

In addition we must also:

- Reflect on how to use technology in connection with the Common Core State Standards

- Realize the need to still teach basic skills and strategies for literacy development.

Teaching Tools and Activities

Assistive Technology (AT)

There is a wide range of Assistive Technology (AT) tools currently available to support students who struggle with reading and literacy skills. Many of these tools assist students in the areas of decoding, reading fluency, comprehension and writing. These types of tools can be useful in the classroom. The following are some of the types of tools currently available:

- Audio Books

  - Audio books via CDs or MP3s allow students to listen to a text being read aloud while they read along with the text. This can help build fluency, word identification and critical listening skills, along with developing better comprehension.

- Screen Readers

  - A software programs that allow users to read the text that is displayed on the computer screen with a speech synthesizer. This is often used for those that are visually impaired, but other products, such as Microsoft's free text-to-speech plug-in named WordTalk, can be used for students with reading disabilities in order to help them understand writings on their computer screen.

- Speech Synthesizers

  - Speech synthesizers are often used to assist those with visual impairments or reading disabilities. Using a computer with text-to-speech software, students can listen to written texts in the form of a human voice.

- Websites and Applications for Better Readability

  - Websites are often very busy with a variety of formatting that can be problematic for some students who have difficulty concentrating when reading online. The Readability product, located at *http://www.readability.com/*, helps turn any web page into a readable site with less clutter and commercials. You can mark to read the website now or later in its new, clean form.

Blogs

A blog is a website on which a student, or sometimes a group of students, can write about ideas and thoughts, personal opinions, or news and information on a recurring and ongoing basis. Blogs are usually posted in reverse chronological order and offer a section for responses. Many teachers see classroom blogs as a way to create an online journal for students to complete certain types or reading and writing assignments. An example of a blog assignment may be to have individual students create an entry on a piece of text or book they've recently read, making sure to give their opinion. Another idea may be to have students write an expository entry regarding certain news or happenings at the school or in the classroom. Peer responses are an important part of a blog because students have to consider not only their own thoughts but also their audiences as well. KidBlog is recognized by many teachers as being the most kid friendly and safe. *http://kidblog.org/home/*

Classroom Wikis

Similar to a blog, a classroom wiki can be useful in developing expository writing and practicing critical thinking skills. One of the key differences between wikis and blogs is that the former allows all members of a group or classroom to have access and to edit the material being posted. Wikis are great for group projects and collaboration or even whole-class activities. A useful idea that incorporates note-taking, reading, and summarizing is to have students create entries involving a collaborative project or report. Allowing students to add their individual thoughts and notes to the group wiki can be a powerful learning experience.

Digital Texts and Digital Libraries

Digital texts are becoming more abundant as mobile reading via tablets and mobile phones are being utilized in daily life. An ebook, electronic-book, offers all of us the ability to access and read a given text almost instantly via downloads and online applications. In addition to digital books and publications there are new focuses on creating digital libraries. Digital libraries contain collections of ebooks, documents, and materials in digital formats that are accessible on computers, tablets and other mobile devices via the Internet. Digital libraries provide access to these books and materials often free of charge to students around the world. Increasing access to digital materials is fundamental to providing opportunities for exploring new literacies and building upon developmental reading skills. Elementary school teachers can use digital libraries for writing resources, research collections, and motivating explorations in literacy. A list of some of the most known and useful digital libraries follows.

- The International Children's Digital Library (ICDL)

    - *http://en.childrenslibrary.org/index.shtml*

- The Smithsonian Digital Library

    - *http://library.si.edu/digital-library*

- StoryPlace: The Children's Digital Library

    - *http://www.storyplace.org/*

- World Digital Library

    - *http://www.wdl.org/en/*

Digital Storytelling, Writing, and Presentation Applications

Storytelling has been part of most cultures since the beginning of mankind. Students enjoy a good story and assisting them with creating, designing, writing, and presenting a story can be very useful for their literacy development. Depending on the specific area being covered in the curriculum, teachers may have their students create narrative type storytelling projects. Other teachers may prefer that students construct an expository or informational type of telling. Many teachers use certain applications geared toward helping students through each stage of a digital storytelling project. The following applications and websites offer ways to create storytelling projects using animations, storyboards, and videos.

Animation/Avatars

- Tellagami: *https://tellagami.com/*

- Voki: *http://www.voki.com/*

- Xtranormal: *http://www.xtranormal.com/*

Create a Video/Movie

- Animoto: *http://animoto.com/*

- Diital Storyteller: *http://www.digitalstoryteller.org/*

- Flowboard: *http://flowboard.com/*

- Meograph: *http://www.meograph.com/*

- WeVideo: *http://www.wevideo.com/education*

Writing/Storyboard

- Amazon Storyteller: *http://studios.amazon.com/storyteller*

- BoomWriter: *http://www.boomwriter.com/home/Schools*

- Penzu: *http://penzu.com/content/products/classroom*

- Storyboard Organizer: *http://storyweb.edublogs.org/files/2010/01/Storyboard-Organizer.pdf*
- Storyboard That: *http://www.storyboardthat.com/*

Glogster *(http://edu.glogster.com/)*

Glogster EDU is an education platform allowing students to create online, multimedia posters using text, photos, videos, graphics, sounds, drawings, and data attachments. This digital tool helps students design their own poster based on whatever topic they wish using digital media. The Glogster posters are then stored online and can be accessible via a link. One idea for intermediate students is to design a Glogster on the topic of regions of the world. Students, individually or in groups, could summarize information about the region, create a video describing the region and culture, and draw a graphic/diagram regarding something about that region. All types of media can be inserted into the Glogster to create a visually insightful project.

Graphic Organizer and Mind Map Software

Using outlining and mapping software can assist students with organizing their thoughts, brainstorming about writing prompts, and connecting concepts together. Products like Inspiration and Kidspiration are well-known for allowing students to create their own organizers or maps that will help with the development of critical thinking skills. One excellent idea for mind mapping is to have students create their own visual venn diagram for comparing and contrasting stories. Another useful example is to have students create a Civil War timeline using this type of software while using their textbook as a guide. Online products like Webspiration and free, java-based products such as Free Mind are also popular in this category.

Tablets and Mobile Applications

Ever hear the phrase, there's an app for that? Well, for the most part there is an app, or application, for almost anything. Whether it be via Apple or Android, mobile technology—tablets, mobile phones, or other portable devices—provides a variety of applications we can use for fun, business, or daily life. This includes the many educational-based apps and those apps created from new technologies.

Finding an app for a mobile device is probably not difficult but deciding if it is useful and appropriate may take a few more steps. The following websites offer rubrics and ideas for evaluating educational applications for mobile devices:

- Ways to Evaluate Educational Apps: *http://learninginhand.com/blog/ways-to-evaluate-educational-apps.html*
- 7 Essential Criteria for Evaluating Mobile Educational Applications: *http://mayraixavillar.wordpress.com/2012/12/06/7-essential-criteria-for-evaluating-mobile-educational-applications/*

Twitter *(https://twitter.com/)*

Twitter deems itself as a real-time, online, information network that connects users to the latest stories, ideas, opinions and news occurring at any given time. Using small bursts of information called Tweets, each Tweet being no more than 140 characters long, users can share small bits of information of their choosing. Primary teachers often choose to create Tweets as a classroom project and share their information with only approved Twitter followers such as parents and other teachers. In the same way as many primary teachers use the Language Experience Approach, the teacher and students would create a Tweet as a class, working through what they wanted to say about their day or about a project that they are working on. Intermediate students may work collaboratively in small groups, or individually to give updates on what they are learning, ask questions about projects, or even summarize a story they have recently read. Some teachers have used Twitter to create an online, educational, scavenger hunt or have had students write a story together using Tweets. As with any social media, teachers will want to make sure it is allowed by their school and/or district to use. Teachers should make sure to use only the first name of students and should not attach personal photos.

Wordle

Wordle is an online application used for generating "word clouds" from text that is provided by students. The word clouds encompass all words but give greater importance to words that are found most often in the source text. Elementary school teachers can create Wordles via their whole class by asking students to brainstorm adjectives to describe a character in a text. Discussion could take place regarding why students feel that some adjectives should be used more based on their feelings about the character and the character's actions. During a social studies lesson students could use Wordle to find the most used words in certain speeches or documents they are studying.

Promoting Independent Reading

What It Is and What Research Can Tell Us

Independent reading is when children read books for pleasure. The ultimate goal of teaching reading is to produce independent, critical, flexible readers, who like to read. This goal is highly prized in American society. All the best intentions and instructions are lost if students cannot apply their abilities to new situations and do not read on their own.

The benefits of independent reading are numerous. Students:

- learn to value reading as both a functional and a leisure-time activity,

- improve their comprehension abilities,

- develop their background knowledge,

- increase their vocabulary knowledge,

- master their decoding skills and abilities, and

- become fluent in their reading.

Independent reading also helps students to improve their reading and writing (Cunningham and Stanovich, 1998).

Students learn reading skills and strategies in the instructional program, and they then practice these same skills and strategies in independent or recreational reading. Students require interesting and varied reading for their abilities to become automatic. For example, the ability to identify new words automatically allows students to devote more attention to deriving meaning from the text. This argument is cyclical; for without abundant practice and becoming fluent in their reading, chances are slim students will read on their own.

In many instances, the classroom time periods devoted to independent reading are known as Sustained Silent Reading (SSR) or Drop Everything And Read (DEAR). However, this independent reading needs to be more than just unfocused, free reading by students. The reading should be purposeful and monitored by the classroom teacher. One such effective modification of independent reading time was designed and implemented by Kelley and Clausen-Grace (2006). Their design, labeled *R5* (read, relax, reflect, respond, and rap), provides an active process for promoting purposeful reading, student involvement, and sharing. In discussing the benefits of *R5*, Kelley and Clausen-Grace state:

> Teachers need to carefully and consistently monitor and guide the developing reading habits of their students. Building in opportunities for sharing ideas and discussions about text can be a powerful motivation for engaging readers. A thoughtful modification of SSR geared to the needs of a class can result in significant gains on formal assessments of wide reading, metacognitive awareness, and comprehension. (pp. 154–155)

Teacher Behaviors

- Select books and other materials for students that are both interesting and easy to read.

- Provide classroom time for students to read independently and at their own pace.

- Provide opportunities for students to discuss their books with both you and their peers.

- Read books aloud to students, stopping to discuss and elaborate on various parts.

- Secure books for students that reflect students' background and cultural heritage.

- Monitor independent reading, and keep records to show the progress of each student.

Teaching Strategies

Book Week Celebration Each Fall Season

An excellent way to foster independent reading is to celebrate Book Week each year. Book Week is sponsored by the Children's Book Council in New York City and is celebrated each November. The Children's Book Council is an excellent source for book project ideas, posters, bookmarks, and a variety of materials related to celebrating books. The following is a summary of an integrated language arts unit to celebrate Book Week.

Introduction

This project is planned around the celebration of Book Week, which occurs during November each year. Work on the whole-class project starts in September, with culminating activities during Book Week, two-and-a-half months later. This highly motivating, integrated, reading/language arts unit can enliven the classroom environment and launch the year in an exciting fashion. The activities that follow are completed periodically during traditional reading, language arts, and art periods.

Activities Prior to Book Week

1. Discuss with students the idea of a class project occurring over two to three months. Emphasize both individual effort and teamwork as crucial to project success. Next, discuss the importance of recreational reading, including different types of books and different authors, and of the allocation of school and outside-of-school time for wide reading or independent reading. Last, administer an interest inventory to all students to help in selecting library books for the classroom.

2. Initiate an intensive recreational reading program as soon as the school year begins, allowing students to read books of their choice. Also, as soon as possible, encourage students to choose their favorite book.

3. Form cooperative learning groups (heterogeneous in ability) to accomplish various purposes in the unit.

4. Have students identify the author of their favorite book and discuss what they would like to tell or ask the author if they had the opportunity to do so. Suggest that, as an entire class project, students should write a letter to their favorite authors. Replies from the authors (and many times the publishers as well) will be proudly displayed during Book Week. Give whole-class instruction on the basics of letter writing. In the cooperative groups, require each student to write a letter to the author of his or

her favorite book. Cooperative groups work together on this activity, during which peer tutoring and cooperation between team members are emphasized. Encourage students to explain to the authors why they liked the books so much, and if they had a question about the story, suggest that students ask the authors for an explanation. Have students write preliminary drafts of their letters, rewrite, and then polish their initial efforts in a team atmosphere. Send the letters by the end of September to ensure responses from the authors and publishers by Book Week.

5. Require a written book report on each student's favorite book (due at the end of October). The written reports should include a summary of the book, ideas and experiences in the book the student would like to share with others, descriptions of main characters, and the most interesting events in the story.

6. To aid in both the written book report and the oral report to be given at the Book Fair, provide direct instruction and much interesting and varied practice in the skills of summarizing, determining the author's purpose, and comparing. The primary vehicles to teach these skills will be students' favorite books. Assignments associated with these skills will be completed in cooperative groups. Members of each group will work together on their books—summarizing the plots and comparing stories, characters, settings, plots, and styles of writing.

7. Have students create dioramas depicting a particular scene from their favorite book. Using cardboard boxes as shells, students may design their own scene with whatever materials are at their disposal.

8. As responses are received from students' favorite authors, show off their personal letters on a bulletin board.

9. In preparation for Book Week, have students practice two plays, giving special attention to public speaking and acting qualities. Examples of plays are *How a Book Is Made* and *How to Use the Library.* The Children's Book Council in New York is an excellent source for suggestions for plays, materials, posters, and Book Fairs to celebrate Book Week.

10. As another instructional activity and bulletin board display before Book Week, ask students to prepare a book jacket and/or bookmark of their favorite book and to compose a telegram summarizing their book in 25 words or less.

11. In preparation for Book Week, have students (in cooperative teams) prepare and practice imaginative oral reports to present along with their dioramas.

12. Invite an author of children's books to speak to your class and the school assembly during Book Week. The appearance of such an author would be an attractive and beneficial addition to the celebration. The author might also observe the work students designed for Book Week.

Activities during Book Week

Activities of the Book Week celebration take place over at least three days. Reserve two days for the display of the dioramas and accompanying oral book reports: one day for visits from other classes in the school and the second day for visits from parents and central office administrators. Each student should be positioned next to his or her diorama and deliver a short oral summary of the diorama and book. In addition, the classroom should be decorated with student-created bulletin boards, as well as various posters and artwork celebrating Book Week. Reserve the third day for the school assembly, featuring the two plays and a short address by a children's book author.

Classroom Ideas to Promote Recreational Reading and Writing

- Read good stories and books aloud to students.

- Discuss with students a book they will be reading.

- Set aside 15 to 30 minutes each day for students to silently read material on their own. At appropriate times, encourage students to write about what they have read.

- Encourage students to react to a story, making predictions and commenting on the story's conclusion.

- Create interest groups around particular topics or books.

- Capitalize on students' interests by carefully selecting the reading materials used for instructional purposes.

- Help students select books by making personal recommendations.

- Share different types of your writing styles (memos, letters) with your students.

- Encourage recreational reading and writing by making a "reading and writing corner" or "reading and writing center" in the classroom.

- Encourage students to use their local library.

- Encourage reading at home by explaining to parents the benefits of reading to their children.

- Invite a storyteller to your classroom or tell stories to your students yourself.

- Encourage students to:

    —write letters to friends and recommend a book.

    —decorate a bulletin board with pictures of people laughing and personal written accounts from funny stories.

    —write a movie script for a good action story and share it with the class.

    —compose a set of questions that they think readers should know.

    —write or tell a humorous incident, the most exciting happening, or the part they liked the best about a favorite book.

    —construct a diorama representing a scene from a story and write a summary of the scene depicted.

    —broadcast a book review to other classes over the school's audio or video system; this activity requires writing, reading, and correct speech.

    —display illustrated maps showing a character's travels or the area a book encompasses.

    —dress as one of the characters in the book and answer questions in an interview or newscast.

—pretend to be a book character and exchange letters with another student who is pretending to be a book character (students write letters to one another as the characters might).

—write a diary or log to represent the experiences of a book's main character.

—construct mobiles consisting either of the major characters from the story or of scenes or the plot.

—make booklets about their favorite authors (including the author's background and other works he or she has written).

—write a thumbnail review of characters to introduce fellow classmates to people they might enjoy getting to know ("You Meet Such Interesting People in Books").

Capsule Review of Reading Skills and Strategies

Basic Content of Word Identification

Phonological Awareness

Rhymes
Alliteration
Syllable awareness
Phoneme deletion
Phoneme segmentation
Phoneme substitution
Analysis of phonemes

Phonics

Consonants:
    Initial
    Medial
    Final
    Consonant blends:
        "r"   *br, cr, dr, fr, gr, pr, tr*
        "l"   *bl, cl, fl, gl, sl*
        Others: *sc, sk, sm, sn, ap, st, sw, dw, tw*
    Consonant digraphs: *th, ph, gh, sh, ch, ng*
    Silent letters: "kn" (*knee*); "ten" (*fasten*)
    Other consonants:
        "c" before *e, i, y* usually sounds like "s"; sounds like "k" elsewhere
        "g" before *e, i, y* usually sounds like "j"; sounds like "g" elsewhere

Vowels:
    Long, short

    Vowel digraphs:
        ai, ea, ee, oa
        oo (as in *cook*), *oo* (as in *moon*)
        au, aw
        eu, ew
"Y" generalizations:

- When "y" is in a closed syllable that has no vowel, it usually records the short "i" sound *(myth)*.

- When "y" is the final sound in a syllable or word, it usually records the long "i" sound *(my)*.

- When "y" is the final sound in a multisyllabic word, it usually records the long "e" sound *(softly)*.

Vowel principles:

- One vowel at the end of a syllable or word is usually long *(he, tulip)*.

- The vowel "e" at the end of a word separated by a consonant is silent, and the vowel in the middle is long *(make)*.

- Two vowels together: First is long, second is silent *(team)*.

- One vowel in the middle of a word is usually short *(tap)*.

- One vowel at the beginning of a word or syllable is usually short *(it)*.

Structural Analysis

Syllabication principles:

- Vowel followed by two consonants—Division often occurs between the consonants *(num ber)*.

- Vowel followed by one consonant and another vowel—Division often occurs before the consonant *(pu pil)*.

- A word ending with "le"—The consonant before plus the "le" form a syllable *(ta ble)*.

- A word containing "x" proceeded and followed by a vowel—Usually, the "x" and the preceding vowel are in one syllable, while the following vowel is in another *(ox en)*.

Other features of syllables:

- When a single vowel is followed by "r," the "r" controls the sound, as in *art, her, for, fir, fur.*

- When "o" is the only vowel and is followed by "ld," it records its long sound *(bold, behold, told, old)*.

- When "a" is followed by double "ll" or "lk," it often sounds like "aw" *(all, balk)*.

- When "i" is the only vowel and is followed by "ld," "nd," "gn," "gh," or "ght," it records the long sound *(mild, kind, sign, sigh, might)*.

Prefixes
Suffixes
Roots
Inflectional endings
Contractions
Compound words

Context

Semantic clues (meaning of other words helps identifying an unknown word)
Syntactic clues (order of words in a sentence aids in identifying an unknown word)

Sight Vocabulary

Personal words; words in the child's first readers; basic service, instant, or high-frequency words occurring in beginning reading materials; and content subject words

Basic Content of Comprehension

Vocabulary Development

- Meaning vocabulary

- Content area words

Literal Comprehension

- Being able to understand facts (who, what, where, when), sequential development (plot structure), story theme, cause-and-effect relationships, fact and opinion

Interpretative or Inferential Comprehension

- Being able to arrive at the main ideas and significant details, make inferences, summarize ideas, perceive relationships and motives of characters' actions, draw conclusions, identify author's purpose and mood

Critical Comprehension

- Being able to critically analyze a story, including hypothesizing, identifying assumptions, imagining, problem solving, comparing and contrasting, applying principles to new situations

- Being able to personally react to a story

Strategic Comprehension

- Being able to apply metacognitive strategies to reading, including prereading strategies (asking questions, setting purposes, making hypotheses), during-reading strategies (knowing when to shift gears—that is, slow down, speed up, skip material, answer purpose-setting questions or hypotheses and set new ones, decide if one is understanding ideas presented or not), and postreading strategies (summarizing ideas, answering purpose-setting questions and verifying hypotheses, reviewing new vocabulary)

Content Area Comprehension

- Knowing how to read a content chapter

- Knowing specific study skills, such as map, table, graph, and chart reading; outlining; use of various reference materials

- Knowing technical vocabulary

- Learning how to apply specific comprehension skills and cognitive strategies to each content area

Explicit/Direct Instruction

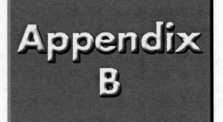

Rationale

Successful reading teachers explicitly or directly teach their students what they need to know; that is, they actually explain, model, or demonstrate a desired objective to students. Teachers have used this approach effectively for a number of years. Educational research overwhelmingly links this teaching approach with increased student achievement (Rosenshine and Stevens, 1995). In the explicit/direct approach, students are taught a new skill or strategy through a planned, structured, systematic explanation and/or modeling; teacher-supervised practice; and an independent practice cycle. In this way, the teacher provides "scaffolded instruction," which helps students to learn a new skill or strategy.

Teaching Steps

1. *Readiness/motivation:* The manner in which the teacher motivates the students, develops the background of the lesson, reviews prior knowledge, and communicates the purpose of the lesson to students.

2. *Teaching:* The manner in which the teacher explains (in a step-by-step fashion, using several examples and counterexamples), models, or demonstrates the new skill or strategy to students. In teaching cognitive strategies, an additional, helpful way to model a strategy to students is through the "think-aloud" technique (that is, telling students how you or any expert reader would perform the strategy at hand while you read).

3. *Guided practice:* A practice activity on the new skill or strategy that students and teacher complete together to ensure students' initial understanding.

4. *Independent practice:* Practice activities in real sentences or in a story on the new skill or strategy that students complete on their own or in a cooperative grouping situation.

5. *Review:* Overall summary and review of the intended instructional objective with additional practice opportunities in whole texts.

Graded Paragraph Inventory (GPI)

An informal reading inventory (IRI), such as the *Graded Paragraph Inventory (GPI)*, is the most beneficial informal reading assessment for the classroom teacher. This inventory should form the central core of assessing both elementary and middle school students' reading abilities. When time is of the essence for initial placement of a student, the GPI assessment is recommended because it can be administered in 15 minutes. The GPI is composed of paragraphs of increasing difficulty or readability. This informal test is given on a one-to-one basis, with the student reading the paragraphs aloud or orally. The major purposes of the GPI are:

1. To determine the student's functional reading levels:

    a. The instructional or "just-right" level, at which the student can complete material with some support from the teacher (challenging but not too difficult). This is the teaching level.

    b. The independent or "easy" level is the highest level at which the student can complete material with no support from the teacher (especially important for assigning homework and books to be read independently).

    c. The frustration or "too difficult" level is the lowest level at which the student cannot handle the material. Of course, this level should be avoided for instruction.

    d. The listening comprehension level is the highest level at which a student can understand 70% of the material read to him or her. The assumption of this informal test is that the student has the potential to read on this level once the teacher matches instruction to the student's strengths and weaknesses.

2. To assess the student's strengths and weaknesses in comprehending text

3. To assess the student's strengths and weaknesses in word identification or decoding

4. To monitor student progress on an ongoing basis

5. To serve as a self-assessment tool for students to become more aware of their own reading strategies and needs

It is imperative that students' functional reading levels be determined. All subsequent instruction (zeroing in on specific learning objectives, focusing on student strengths and weaknesses, executing appropriate teaching techniques and strategies, selecting instructional materials) flows from determining students' instructional reading level. Without constant attention to this concern, successful instruction and learning are unlikely.

Levels

The GPI has one passage for levels preprimer through eighth grade:

- Preprimer
- Primer
- Level 1 (First grade)
- Level 2 (Second grade)
- Level 3 (Third grade)
- Level 4 (Fourth grade)
- Level 5 (Fifth grade)
- Level 6 (Sixth grade)
- Level 7 (Seventh grade)
- Level 8 (Eighth grade)

Administration of Graded Paragraph Inventory

Pretest

1. Drop back three grade levels below the student's present grade placement as a starting point for beginning the inventory.

2. Explain the testing procedure and purpose of the test to the student.

3. Use the first passage as a sample to familiarize the student with the procedure.

4. Discuss the topic of the passage, and review background knowledge with the student.

5. Ask the student to read the passage aloud. Since this is a sample passage and most probably at an easy level, you do not need to record the student's oral reading performance.

6. After the student finishes reading the passage orally, remove the passage, and explain and demonstrate the retelling technique to assess comprehension by applying the "Comprehension Check Template" (provided later in this section), which uses the key question words of *who, what, when, where, how,* and *why.* If the student's responses are incomplete, ask the probing question, "Can you tell me more?"

7. Tell the student that the same procedure will be used with each passage. Be sure that the student is adequately prepared for this testing procedure.

Testing

1. Begin with the passage that is two grade levels below the student's current grade placement.

2. Discuss the topic of the passage, and review background knowledge with the student.

3. Ask the student to read the passage aloud.

4. Pronounce the proper nouns in each passage for the student; do not count as miscues mispronunciation of names in the passages.

5. As the student is reading, record any oral reading miscues and symptoms (see the section "Oral Reading Marking System" later in this appendix). Only miscues are counted in determining word recognition percentage.

6. After the student finishes reading the passage orally, remove the passage, and assess the student's comprehension, using the retelling technique with the "Comprehension Check Template."

7. If, in your estimation, the student understood at least 70% of the passage, (instructional or independent—see the "Composite Scoring Guide" section later in this appendix), continue on to the next passage, and repeat steps 1 through 6.

8. When the student fails to meet the minimum criteria for comprehension (i.e., reaches the frustration level for comprehension, understands less than 70%), the oral reading portion of the inventory is completed. To help in efficiently assessing a student's performance on each passage, a "Composite Scoring Guide" is provided with tabulations already completed. The scoring standard used for word recognition and comprehension is presented in the section "Reading Level Criteria." Also, an explanation for determining both the word recognition and comprehension scores is provided in the section "Scoring Guide."

9. After determining the student's frustration level, read the next passage aloud to the student. Remind the student to listen and try to understand the passage. After reading the passage to the student, ask the comprehension questions in the "Comprehension Check Template." If the student understands at least 70% of the paragraph, go on to the next passage. Repeat the process until the student fails to understand 70% of the passage. The highest or last level at which the student can satisfactorily understand the passage that you read to him or her is considered the student's listening comprehension level.

10. After completion of the inventory, return to each passage and summarize both the word recognition and comprehension findings, and complete the "Graded Paragraph Inventory Summary Form."

Oral Reading Marking System

Miscues		Marking System
Pronunciation (student does not know the word)	P store	Write "P" over the unknown word.
Substitution (student substitutes one real word for another)	snip store	Write the substituted word ("snip") or put an "S" over the word for which the student inserted the substitution ("store").
Mispronunciation (student mispronounces a word)	stip store	Write phonetically how the student mispronounced the word over the actual word, or put "MP" over the actual word.
Insertion (student says a word that is not in print)	big the ˄store	Add a carrot (^) and write the word the student inserted.
Omission (student omits a word)	(the) store	Circle the word omitted.
Reversal (student reverses two words)	he said	Draw a curved line between the two words.

Symptoms (not counted as a miscue)

Self-correction	✓ store	Place a check mark above the word corrected.
Repetition	‾‾‾ store	Draw a straight line over the word repeated.

11. The last (or highest) level at which the student passes the comprehension criterion is the student's instructional level. The frustration or too difficult level is one level higher than the instructional level, and the independent or easy level is one level below the instructional level. The listening

comprehension level is the highest level at which the student understood at least 70% of the passage read to her or him. For example, if the instructional level is determined to be 3, then the frustration level is 4, the independent level is 2, and the listening comprehension level is at least 3. (*Caution:* At times, clear-cut levels are not found. In such cases, use personal information regarding the student and the student's oral reading symptoms at the various levels to help in initially deciding upon the reading levels.)

Comprehension Check Template

Teacher: "Tell me about what you just read." Student should address the following:

_____   Who (is the story about?)
_____   What (happened in the story?)
_____   When (did the story take place?)
_____   Where (did the story take place?)
_____   How (did the story begin and end?)
_____   Why (did something happen?)

Note: Not every passage has an answer for all of the previous questions. Determine if the student can address a sufficient amount of information before proceeding as follows:

0–3 = Frustration level (Stop here—Unsatisfactory)
4–5 = Instruction level (Satisfactory)
6   = Independent level (Excellent)

Reading Level Criteria

Word Recognition	Comprehension
Independent (97–100%)	Independent (90–100%)
Instructional (90–96%, pre-primer level through level 2; 94–96%, level 3 and higher)	Instructional (70–89%)
Frustration (89% and below, preprimer level through level 2; 93% and below, level 3 and higher)	Frustration (below 70%)
	Listening (last level at 70%)

Scoring Guide

Word Recognition

Word recognition percentage is determined by dividing the total number of miscues in the paragraph by the total number of words, multiplying the answer by 100, and subtracting from 100 percent.

Example: Given 3 miscues and a total of 52 words:

$$3 \div 52 = .058 \text{ (round to .06)}$$
$$06 \times 100 = 6\%$$
$$100\% - 6\% = 94\%$$

Comprehension

Using the "Comprehension Check Template" as a guide, estimate the student's understanding of the six key question words (*who, what, when, where, how,* and *why*). Complete understanding of the paragraph would indicate the independent level, one to two errors instructional, and three errors or more frustration level. Your estimate of the student's understanding (unsatisfactory, satisfactory, excellent) is the standard.

For easy scoring, a "Composite Scoring Guide" is provided following each paragraph on the examiner's copy so that you can indicate summary results of error computation.

Graded Paragraph Inventory Summary Form

1. Reading levels:

Instructional level _____

Independent level _____

Frustration level _____

Listening comprehension level _____

2. Student's overall strength:

_____

_____

_____

3. Most common oral reading miscue:

_____

_____

_____

4. Most common comprehension difficulty:

_____

_____

_____

5. Did the student have difficulty with any of the following?

	Yes	No
Fluency	_____	_____
Sight words	_____	_____
Applying phonic or letter/sound knowledge to decode words	_____	_____
Recalling details	_____	_____
Inferring information	_____	_____
Using context clues to confirm his or her attempts at pronouncing words	_____	_____
Drawing upon his or her own personal knowledge to infer information	_____	_____

Graded Paragraph Inventory: Examiner's Copy

Preprimer (45 words)

My Dog Daisy

I have a dog.
Daisy is my dog.
My dog is white and little.
My dog is funny.
I like to play with my dog.
When I say, "Daisy bark," she barks.
When I say, "Daisy sit," she sits.
My dog is a good dog.

Composite Scoring Guide

Word Recognition	Comprehension	Level
0–1 miscue	0 questions missed	Independent
2–3 miscues	1–2 questions missed	Instructional
4+ miscues	3+ questions missed	Frustration

Did the student pass comprehension? If yes, go on to the next level.

Summary of Comprehension Performance

Unsatisfactory _____   Satisfactory _____   Excellent _____

Summary of Word Recognition Performance

Type and number of oral reading miscues:

Pronunciations _____   Insertions _____
Substitutions _____   Omissions _____
Mispronunciations _____   Reversals _____
How many miscues changed the meaning of the sentence? _____

Primer (50 words)

The Movies

"We are going to the movies," said Jill. "It will be a fun day," said Tim. "We will see two movies and have popcorn." Jill said, "It is far away, so we must ride a bus to get there." "I'm ready to go!" said Tim.

Composite Scoring Guide

Word Recognition	Comprehension	Level
0–1 miscue	0 questions missed	Independent
2–3 miscues	1–2 questions missed	Instructional
4+ miscues	3+ questions missed	Frustration

Did the student pass comprehension? If yes, go on to the next level.

Summary of Comprehension Performance

Unsatisfactory _____   Satisfactory _____   Excellent _____

Summary of Word Recognition Performance

Type and number of oral reading miscues:

Pronunciations _____   Insertions _____
Substitutions _____   Omissions _____
Mispronunciations _____   Reversals _____
How many miscues changed the meaning of the sentence? _____

Level 1 (54 words)

BBQ

"I love BBQ," said Wyatt. "Joe cooks chicken and ribs in a big cooker. I go with my friends to see Joe. It is not far from my house. The BBQ smells good. Joe always says hello to me. Joe says, 'I have the best BBQ.' Joe always says, 'Wyatt, come and get it!'"

Composite Scoring Guide

Word Recognition	Comprehension	Level
0–1 miscue	0 questions missed	Independent
2–3 miscues	1–2 questions missed	Instructional
4+ miscues	3+ questions missed	Frustration

Did the student pass comprehension? If yes, go on to the next level.

Summary of Comprehension Performance

Unsatisfactory _____   Satisfactory _____   Excellent _____

Summary of Word Recognition Performance

Type and number of oral reading miscues:

Pronunciations _____   Insertions _____
Substitutions _____   Omissions _____
Mispronunciations _____   Reversals _____
How many miscues changed the meaning of the sentence? _____

Level 2 (93 words)

BB's Store

Andrew loves BB's store. "The store is near my school," said Andrew. "I go to BB's store after school. BB has lots of things in his store. I like to get a juice. BB always says, 'How was school today?' I always tell him about my teacher. Sometimes I stay at the store and talk to BB. He is so nice. My mom and dad go to BB's store too. BB has lots of things in his store. When I leave the store, BB always says, 'Be good, Andrew, and see you tomorrow.'"

Composite Scoring Guide

Word Recognition	Comprehension	Level
0–1 miscue	0 questions missed	Independent
2–3 miscues	1–2 questions missed	Instructional
4+ miscues	3+ questions missed	Frustration

Did the student pass comprehension? If yes, go on to the next level.

Summary of Comprehension Performance

Unsatisfactory _____   Satisfactory _____   Excellent _____

Summary of Word Recognition Performance

Type and number of oral reading miscues:

Pronunciations   _____   Insertions _____
Substitutions   _____   Omissions _____
Mispronunciations _____   Reversals _____
How many miscues changed the meaning of the sentence? _____

Level 3 (113 words)
Weekends

Weekends are so much fun to me. I like them the best. There are so many things to do. Sometimes I go to the movies. Sometimes I go to the park and play lots of games. I like the swings and slides at the playground. Some weekends I go shopping at the mall with my parents and have lunch. Other times we go to the city. We walk around the lake and see the ducks. We go to our grandmother's house and play in the yard. Sometimes we bake cookies. We always go to church and visit with friends. I wish weekends could last longer. They are so busy, but they are fun.

Composite Scoring Guide

Word Recognition	Comprehension	Level
0–1 miscue	0 questions missed	Independent
2–3 miscues	1–2 questions missed	Instructional
4+ miscues	3+ questions missed	Frustration

Did the student pass comprehension? If yes, go on to the next level.

Summary of Comprehension Performance

Unsatisfactory _____   Satisfactory _____   Excellent _____

Summary of Word Recognition Performance

Type and number of oral reading miscues:

Pronunciations _____   Insertions _____
Substitutions _____   Omissions _____
Mispronunciations _____   Reversals _____
How many miscues changed the meaning of the sentence? _____

Level 4 (128 words)

Jazz Camp

"I love to sing and dance," said Donna. "I do too," said Tara. This summer the community center is going to have a Jazz and Dance Camp for the months of June and July. "All of my friends in my school are going to the camp," said Donna. "The director of the camp will play songs we hear on the radio," said Tara. Everyone will learn new dances and have lots of time to practice. Tara said, "My friends and I will get a T-shirt, and we will have refreshments at the end of the day." At the end of the Jazz and Dance Camp, all the dancers will perform new dances for their parents and friends on the stage. "I just can't wait for summer!" said Donna.

Composite Scoring Guide

Word Recognition	Comprehension	Level
0–1 miscue	0 questions missed	Independent
2–3 miscues	1–2 questions missed	Instructional
4+ miscues	3+ questions missed	Frustration

Did the student pass comprehension? If yes, go on to the next level.

Summary of Comprehension Performance

Unsatisfactory _____   Satisfactory _____   Excellent _____

Summary of Word Recognition Performance

Type and number of oral reading miscues:

Pronunciations _____   Insertions _____
Substitutions _____   Omissions _____
Mispronunciations _____   Reversals _____
How many miscues changed the meaning of the sentence? _____

Level 5 (166 words)

The Community Center

Carson goes to the community center every day after school. "I can play outside or inside," says Carson. Sometimes he makes things in the arts and crafts room or does his homework. Sometimes he plays pool, plays games, or watches TV. Other times he goes to the computer room or library. His friends also like to go to the center. There is always someone to help you. Bill is the supervisor of the center. He always says hello to everyone who comes in the front door. He is very nice. Sometimes Carson helps him clean up a room or move tables and chairs. Bill will say, "It's time to put away the tables for the dance class." Carson loves to help at the center. Adults come to the center to exercise, use the weight room, play tennis, and meet with friends. Sometimes a church group will meet at the center. Outside the center there is a playground and swimming pool. It is a fun place to go.

Composite Scoring Guide

Word Recognition	Comprehension	Level
0–1 miscue	0 questions missed	Independent
2–3 miscues	1–2 questions missed	Instructional
4+ miscues	3+ questions missed	Frustration

Did the student pass comprehension? If yes, go on to the next level.

Summary of Comprehension Performance

Unsatisfactory _____   Satisfactory _____   Excellent _____

Summary of Word Recognition Performance

Type and number of oral reading miscues:

Pronunciations _____   Insertions _____
Substitutions _____   Omissions _____
Mispronunciations _____   Reversals _____
How many miscues changed the meaning of the sentence? _____

Level 6 (191words)
Best Friends

Christian is my best friend. We have known each other for five years. We live in the same neighborhood and walk to school together each day. In school, we have had the same teacher for the past three years. We always help each other out both in school and after school. In our classroom, sometimes we do projects together, and we always help each other with our homework. If I am sick, Christian always brings me my homework, and I do the same for him. If I ever need something, he is always there to help me. Once, I needed help bringing home groceries from the store, and he carried a large bag including the heavy soda. On the weekends, we usually go to the park or community center together. It is so wonderful to have a close friend to play games with and just hang out together and listen to our favorite music. My mom likes Christian very much. She likes to make a big supper and invite Christian over to eat. Friends are great to have, and Christian is the best friend I ever had.

Composite Scoring Guide

Word Recognition	Comprehension	Level
0–1 miscue	0 questions missed	Independent
2–3 miscues	1–2 questions missed	Instructional
4+ miscues	3+ questions missed	Frustration

Did the student pass comprehension? If yes, go on to the next level.

Summary of Comprehension Performance

Unsatisfactory _____   Satisfactory _____   Excellent _____

Summary of Word Recognition Performance

Type and number of oral reading miscues:

Pronunciations _____   Insertions _____
Substitutions _____   Omissions _____
Mispronunciations _____   Reversals _____
How many miscues changed the meaning of the sentence? _____

Level 7 (186 words)
The Big Game

It's the weekend, and the big football game is tonight. The sights and sounds surrounding the game are so exciting and special. Every September, October, and November, weekends are busy with family and friends preparing to go to the game. It's important to go to the football game early to meet with friends, to have a hot dog or hamburger and a drink, to get a good seat, and to see all the entertainment. The bands play the school songs, and the cheerleaders perform their cheers and dances. The football players and coaches rush onto the field and warm up for the big game as the fans cheer from the stands. At the beginning of the game, the referees and the team captains meet at midfield for the coin toss to decide which team will begin with the ball. At halftime, it's time for refreshments, visits with family and friends, and watching the bands perform on the field. Of course, if your team wins, it is the best. Even if your team loses, game night is a special event for all the fans.

Composite Scoring Guide

Word Recognition	Comprehension	Level
0–1 miscue	0 questions missed	Independent
2–3 miscues	1–2 questions missed	Instructional
4+ miscues	3+ questions missed	Frustration

Did the student pass comprehension? If yes, go on to the next level.

Summary of Comprehension Performance

Unsatisfactory _____   Satisfactory _____   Excellent _____

Summary of Word Recognition Performance

Type and number of oral reading miscues:

Pronunciations _____   Insertions _____
Substitutions _____   Omissions _____
Mispronunciations _____   Reversals _____
How many miscues changed the meaning of the sentence? _____

Level 8 Narrative (179 words)

Career Day

Every year our school has a "career day." Different people come to our school and talk to us about jobs and the importance of going to college. This year, we had three main speakers. First, the mayor of the city talked to us about representing and serving the citizens of the city, state, and nation. I didn't realize all the responsibilities of an elected official. Second, a software engineer discussed his job and the future that computers will play in our lives. This engineer worked for a company that developed new computer programs for operating the space shuttle in Florida. Third, a professor from the university talked to us about becoming a teacher in our public schools. Teachers are so influential in our lives. The professor said that we would not have top mayors or engineers if we did not have excellent teachers to teach our children in our schools. I think I am still deciding what I would like to do when I finish school. However, it is good to hear about different jobs.

Composite Scoring Guide

Word Recognition	Comprehension	Level
0–1 miscue	0 questions missed	Independent
2–3 miscues	1–2 questions missed	Instructional
4+ miscues	3+ questions missed	Frustration

Did the student pass comprehension? If yes, go on to the next level.

Summary of Comprehension Performance

Unsatisfactory _____   Satisfactory _____   Excellent _____

Summary of Word Recognition Performance

Type and number of oral reading miscues:

Pronunciations _____   Insertions _____
Substitutions _____   Omissions _____
Mispronunciations _____   Reversals _____
How many miscues changed the meaning of the sentence? _____

Graded Paragraph Inventory: Student's Copy

My Dog Daisy

I have a dog.

Daisy is my dog.

My dog is white and little.

My dog is funny.

I like to play with my dog.

When I say, "Daisy bark," she barks.

When I say, "Daisy sit," she sits.

My dog is a good dog.

The Movies

"We are going to the movies," said Jill. "It will be a fun day," said Tim. "We will see two movies and have popcorn." Jill said, "It is far away, so we must ride a bus to get there." "I'm ready to go!" said Tim.

BBQ

"I love BBQ," said Wyatt. "Joe cooks chicken and ribs in a big cooker. I go with my friends to see Joe. It is not far from my house. The BBQ smells good. Joe always says hello to me. Joe says, 'I have the best BBQ.' Joe always says, 'Wyatt, come and get it!'"

BB's Store

Andrew loves BB's store. "The store is near my school," said Andrew. "I go to BB's store after school. BB has lots of things in his store. I like to get a juice. BB always says, 'How was school today?' I always tell him about my teacher. Sometimes I stay at the store and talk to BB. He is so nice. My mom and dad go to BB's store too. BB has lots of things in his store. When I leave the store, BB always says, 'Be good, Andrew, and see you tomorrow.'"

Weekends

Weekends are so much fun to me. I like them the best. There are so many things to do. Sometimes I go to the movies. Sometimes I go to the park and play lots of games. I like the swings and slides at the playground. Some weekends I go shopping at the mall with my parents and have lunch. Other times we go to the city. We walk around the lake and see the ducks. We go to our grandmother's house and play in the yard. Sometimes we bake cookies. We always go to church and visit with friends. I wish weekends could last longer. They are so busy, but they are fun.

Jazz Camp

"I love to sing and dance," said Donna. "I do too," said Tara. This summer the community center is going to have a Jazz and Dance Camp for the months of June and July. "All of my friends in my school are going to the camp," said Donna. "The director of the camp will play songs we hear on the radio," said Tara. Everyone will learn new dances and have lots of time to practice. Tara said, "My friends and I will get a T-shirt, and we will have refreshments at the end of the day." At the end of the Jazz and Dance Camp, all the dancers will perform new dances for their parents and friends on the stage. "I just can't wait for summer!" said Donna.

The Community Center

Carson goes to the community center every day after school. "I can play outside or inside," says Carson. Sometimes he makes things in the arts and crafts room or does his homework. Sometimes he plays pool, plays games, or watches TV. Other times he goes to the computer room or library. His friends also like to go to the center. There is always someone to help you. Bill is the supervisor of the center. He always says hello to everyone who comes in the front door. He is very nice. Sometimes Carson helps him clean up a room or move tables and chairs. Bill will say, "It's time to put away the tables for the dance class." Carson loves to help at the center. Adults come to the center to exercise, use the weight room, play tennis, and meet with friends. Sometimes a church group will meet at the center. Outside the center there is a playground and swimming pool. It is a fun place to go.

Best Friends

Christian is my best friend. We have known each other for five years. We live in the same neighborhood and walk to school together each day. In school, we have had the same teacher for the past three years. We always help each other out both in school and after school. In our classroom, sometimes we do projects together, and we always help each other with our homework. If I am sick, Christian always brings me my homework, and I do the same for him. If I ever need something, he is always there to help me. Once, I needed help bringing home groceries from the store, and he carried a large bag including the heavy soda. On the weekends, we usually go to the park or community center together. It is so wonderful to have a close friend to play games with and just hang out together and listen to our favorite music. My mom likes Christian very much. She likes to make a big supper and invite Christian over to eat. Friends are great to have, and Christian is the best friend I ever had.

The Big Game

It's the weekend, and the big football game is tonight. The sights and sounds surrounding the game are so exciting and special. Every September, October, and November, weekends are busy with family and friends preparing to go the game. It's important to go to the football game early to meet with friends, to have a hot dog or hamburger and a drink, to get a good seat, and to see all the entertainment. The bands play the school songs, and the cheerleaders perform their cheers and dances. The football players and coaches rush onto the field and warm up for the big game as the fans cheer from the stands. At the beginning of the game, the referees and the team captains meet at midfield for the coin toss to decide which team will begin with the ball. At halftime, it's time for refreshments, visits with family and friends, and watching the bands perform on the field. Of course, if your team wins, it is the best. Even if your team loses, game night is a special event for all the fans.

Career Day

Every year our school has a "career day." Different people come to our school and talk to us about jobs and the importance of going to college. This year, we had three main speakers. First, the mayor of the city talked to us about representing and serving the citizens of the city, state, and nation. I didn't realize all the responsibilities of an elected official. Second, a software engineer discussed his job and the future that computers will play in our lives. This engineer worked for a company that developed new computer programs for operating the space shuttle in Florida. Third, a professor from the university talked to us about becoming a teacher in our public schools. Teachers are so influential in our lives. The professor said that we would not have top mayors or engineers if we did not have excellent teachers to teach our children in our schools. I think I am still deciding what I would like to do when I finish school. However, it is good to hear about different jobs.

Parent Guide:
Helping Your Child Become a Better Reader

Appendix D

The age-old expression "Reading begins in the home" is entirely correct. As parents (and grandparents), you are your child's first teacher, and you play a crucial role in laying the foundation for reading success. The ability to read is linked to success in all school subjects and to success later on in life. You are the one who supports and guides your child through a variety of experiences and helps your child to express ideas with words and to understand what words mean. As your child progresses in school, your expectations and actions continue to influence how much and how well he or she reads. Family members have a significant impact on a child's reading achievement.

What is reading? Reading is comprehending or understanding. In the early stages of learning to read, children learn letters, sounds, individual words, and other skills needed to identify and interpret an unknown word. They also learn other specific skills to understand the ideas or thoughts represented by the letters and words. Learning to read takes time and effort. Children don't suddenly read entire books—learning to read involves learning one step at a time, followed by meaningful practice and lots of recreational reading. In this way, learning to read is similar to learning a new skill like riding a bicycle or learning how to drive a car. However, it is important to remember that to read is to understand—without understanding or comprehension, there is no reading.

The suggestions here will help you guide your child to improve his or her reading skills. Remember, you are a key person in whether or not your child will experience success in reading. You can help control your child's feelings about learning to read, support the instruction your child is receiving in school, teach your child specific reading skills, and then practice those skills in the home. You can help your child improve his or her reading at home even if you yourself had some difficulties in learning to read. You don't have to be an expert. Use the information in this guide as suggestions, and then go ahead and do the best you can.

Most children will learn how to read. Whether they will become good readers depends in large part on your help and encouragement. Show your child that reading is important by having them see you read magazines, newspapers, church bulletins, and books—remember, your child will copy what you do. Try to make all reading activities in the home fun. Be positive, even if an activity is not going well. In such cases, stop and try the activity again at some later time.

Here are 10 ways for you to help your child become a better reader:*

1. *Help children acquire a wide range of knowledge.* When you take your children on shopping trips, walks in the park, and visits to zoos and museums, you help give them the important background knowledge they will need as they learn to read school textbooks. Children's ability to understand even simple stories can depend on their having both common and not-so-common knowledge.

2. *Talk with children about their experiences.* When you talk with children about their experiences, you help them learn new words and understand what these new words mean. Talking with children also helps them learn from their experiences and use this new knowledge to understand what they are reading. As a result, they will better understand what they are reading.

3. *Encourage children to think about events.* Ask your children to describe events. This makes them reflect on experiences and helps them learn to give good descriptions

---

*From "10 Ways to Help Your Child Become a Better Reader," Center for the Study of Reading, University of Illinois, n.d.

and tell complete stories. These activities help children to better understand how stories are written and what they are reading.

4. *Read aloud to children.* Reading aloud is probably the single most important activity you can do to encourage children's success as readers. It is an especially important activity during the preschool years. When you read lots of stories to children, and look at lots of picture books with them, you help them build the store of knowledge they will use when they begin to read in school. The benefits of reading aloud are greatest when you encourage children to participate by identifying letters and words and talking about the story and the meaning of words.

5. *Provide preschool children with writing materials.* Writing is an important way for children to learn about letters and words. Children are often very eager to learn how to write, and you can encourage them by having paper and pencils or crayons in your home and helping them when they start drawing letters. Even when children are too young to hold a pencil or crayon, you can use devices such as magnetic boards and letters to help them learn about letters and words.

6. *Encourage children to watch TV programs that have educational value.* Watching television programs that teach about reading and language can positively affect children's learning. You can make sure they watch these programs regularly. You can also help them learn from these programs by asking questions about the shows and relating what they are seeing to other situations and experiences.

7. *Monitor how much TV children watch.* Watching quality television programs up to about 10 hours a week can have a slightly positive effect on children's achievement in school, including their reading achievement. As the number of hours of viewing per week increases, however, TV watching becomes a negative influence on children's schoolwork. Most children who watch television 20 or more hours a week do not do well in school.

8. *Monitor children's school performance.* When you visit your children's teachers, observe their classrooms, find out about the reading programs in their schools, and participate in home-school programs, you get a good idea of how your children are doing in school and how you can help them become better students. Research shows that children tend to be more successful readers when their parents have an accurate view of their schoolwork.

9. *Encourage children to read independently.* The amount of reading children do outside of school influences how well they will read in school. Must American children don't read very much during their free time. One of your top priorities as a parent should be to encourage children to spend more time reading. You can help them read more by having plenty of books in your home and visiting the library regularly.

10. *Continue your personal involvement in children's growth as readers.* Set a good example for children by reading newspapers, magazines, and books. Suggest reading as a leisure-time activity, and make sure children have time for reading. You may want, for example, to establish a bedtime hour after which reading is the only activity permitted other than going to sleep.

Communicating High Expectations to Your Children

By following the 10 suggestions in the previous section, you not only are showing children that you want them to be good readers; you also are communicating that you "expect" them to do well in school and in learning to read. Parental attitudes and expectations about how well children can and should perform in school can have a powerful effect on the eventual outcome. You want to hold high expectations for children and communicate these expectations to them. Low expectations are likely to interfere with children successfully learning to read. So, how can you make sure you are holding and communicating high expectations for your child? Here are a few tips:

- Tell children each day that you have faith in them, that they are improving, and that they will be successful in school that very day.

- In the evening, ask children about their day, and praise them for listening to their teachers and working hard in school. Even on those days where everything did not go well in school, remind children that we all have bad days. Communicate that they are doing well and are improving, and that you are proud of their efforts and of them.

- Monitor children's homework each day, and praise them for their good work. If children are experiencing a problem with an assignment, sit down with them and try to help.

- Have a special interest in "attention to detail." Ask children what book they are reading in class and what reading skills they are learning in school. Have children show you their schoolwork, and check to see if children are completing the work neatly and completely. Tell children that you can tell they are improving in reading and how smart they are.

- Make a progress chart listing each book children read, and attach it to the refrigerator.

- At the end of each week, talk to children about school and what new things they learned. Tell them what a great week they had and that you are proud of them.

Specific Reading Techniques to Increase Children's Reading Ability

To become successful readers, children learn and practice new reading skills in school each day. Your child's teacher is helping your child become a good reader by teaching needed reading skills in a specific manner. You can support the instruction children are receiving in school by asking the teacher what you can do at home to reinforce what your child is learning in school. *In this way, you can help teach your child to read at home.* The following important areas are discussed next, with specific recommendations to help you teach children to improve their reading abilities at home: (1) teaching new sight words, (2) helping children become aware of individual sounds in words, (3) teaching letter or vowel sounds—phonics, (4) reading a story or book with children, (5) improving children's ability to comprehend or understand ideas, and (6) helping children to read quickly and smoothly.

Teaching a New Sight Word to Children

Students need to learn many words in our language "by sight"—that is, recognize them instantly. Sight vocabulary is comprised of common words in our language that make up a significant percentage of words read each day. Once children can recognize many words "by sight" or automatically, they can devote more time to thinking about and comprehending ideas in the story.

Sight words are taught by using the whole-word approach (sometimes called the sight-word approach). In this approach, students learn a word by looking at it as a whole, not by dissecting it letter by letter. Ask your child's teacher for sight word lists or "Google" *sight word lists* on the Internet. Choose about five words your child does not know, and teach them in 15 to 20 minutes (don't spend too long if some words are difficult—remember, tomorrow is another day!). Here are the steps to follow in teaching a sight word at home:

- Write the word to be learned on a sheet of paper or a 3-inch-by-5-inch card. Say the word aloud, and make sure your child is looking at the word as you say it.

- Say the word in a sentence to your child.

- Pronounce the word over and over for your child, and then have your child pronounce the word over and over. Use the word in different sentences, and then have your child use the word in different sentences.

- Play games with this sight word and others. For example, you can play "bingo" or "climb the ladder." In "climb the ladder," draw a ladder on a sheet of paper and place or write sight words on each rung of the ladder. Children "climb" to the top of the ladder by pronouncing each word and using it in a sentence.

- The next day, always review the words you taught the previous day. Sometimes, children need a little extra practice.

Ask your child's teacher for sight-word lists to help in your teaching, or use a search engine on the Internet to locate these lists. Play many games and activities with children to practice words so that children will know the words "on sight" or automatically. The following are examples of word games and activities you can play with children:

- Make a chart of happy words and phrases.

- Brainstorm with children in making up word lists of general categories, such as shapes, colors, sports, etc.

- Have children write sight words on strips of paper, hang the strips on coat hangers, and hang the coat hangers from the ceiling. Periodically, have children pronounce the words, write the words, and use them in a sentence.

- Write new words on a card or sheet of paper, and put these new words in a bag or box. Every day or two, take out the words, and ask children to pronounce the words and use them in a sentence.

- Show children the grocery list, pronounce each word, and ask children to pronounce their favorite words.

- Don't forget other important sources of learning and practicing sight words, like the Yellow Pages in a telephone directory, store catalogs, the sports page from the local newspaper, local community center flyers, words for a popular song, and church publications.

Helping Children Learn about Sounds in Language

Children need to learn that spoken sentences are made up of words and that words are made up of separate, individual sounds. Phonemic awareness is the understanding that words in the English language are made up of a sequence of individual, connected sounds or phonemes. For example, "cat" is made up of three connected sounds—*c, a,* and *t.* The quality of phonemic awareness is a major predictor of success in becoming a successful reader in not only first grade but beyond. First-graders lacking this quality have extreme difficulty in being successful in traditional phonics instruction. Many students have little difficulty with phonemic awareness. Being read to and informally playing with words in the home and in preschools teaches students about sounds and letters. Here are some specific ways to promote phonemic awareness at home:

- *Recognizing words with the same sound.* Give children a set of words—for example: *cat, dog,* and *cake.* Ask them to say the words aloud. Then have them say the words that have the same beginning sound. You may want to ask children what the beginning sound is. Do this several times.

- *Isolating sounds.* Show children a list of words. Focus on one word at a time. For example, show the word *dog* and ask children to say the beginning sound of the word. You can do this with the first and last sound in a word. Make sure you do this several times with other words.

- *Deleting sounds.* Help children learn to separate sounds at the beginning of words. For example, ask what would be left if you took the *h* sound out of *hat* or the *p* sound out of *pin.*

- *Identification of rhyming words.* Teach children to pick out rhyming words through the repetition of songs, poems, nursery rhymes, and chants. Read a rhyming book over and over with children. Ask if they notice anything. Make sure to point out the rhyming at the end of the line. Read the passage a second time, but this time, have children raise their hand every time they hear a rhyming word.

- *Syllable recognition.* Say a word and have children clap out each syllable. For example, the word *playground* has two syllables: play-ground.

- *Use of practical or real-life materials.* Don't forget to use materials like the Yellow Pages, store catalogs, cereal box toy offers, the sports page from the local newspaper, local community center flyers, words for a popular song, and church publications for highlighting and practicing various language sounds with children.

Phonics: Teaching a Letter Sound or Vowel Sound to Children

In the English language, written words represent a collection of speech sounds. Phonics is a system of teaching letter–sound relationships and their pronunciations so students can pronounce unknown words on their own. For example, the nonsense word *zoat* is pronounced like *boat.* In these two words, when two vowels are together in a word, you pronounce the long sound of the first vowel and the second vowel is silent or is not pronounced. Ask your child's teacher for phonic word lists to help in your teaching, or "Google" *phonic word lists* on the Internet to locate them. The basic procedure for teaching a phonic element is to use lots of examples illustrating the letter or sound and help children "discover" the letter or sound. Here are the steps to follow at home in teaching relationships involving the initial sound of *b* and the long sound of the vowel letter *a.*

The sound of b:
*   Write and say words that begin with *b* that children already knows by sight—for example, *ball, bat, and bell*.

*   Ask children what is alike about the words, and hopefully, they will discover that the words contain the letter *b,* which represents the *b* sound.

*   Ask for more words that begin with the *b* sound.

*   Both you and the children should take turns using the *b* words in sentences.

*   Read a book and ask children to raise their hand upon hearing a word that begins with the *b* sound.

The long sound of a:
*   Write and say words that have the long sound of *a* in them—or example, *cake, ate, face,* and *make*.

*   Ask children what sound of the vowel *a* do they hear.

*   Ask for more words with the long *a* sound.

*   Both you and the children should take turns using the words in sentences.

*   Read a book together, and ask children to raise their hand upon hearing a word that has the long *a* sound.

After explaining a phonic skill, make sure to have children practice the new skill in sentences, using a variety of games and activities. By practicing the new skill many times, children are able to use the skill in their reading. The following are some games and activities that you can do with children to practice a phonic skill:

*   *Matching pictures and words.* Show a picture of an object and follow it by four words, none of which names the picture but one or more of which begin with the same sound as the name of the pictured object. Ask children to draw a circle around the words that begin with the same sound. You can do this with final consonant sounds as well.

*   *Shopping exercise.* When going with you to the grocery store or the mall, have children sound out the words on your shopping list.

*   *Food packages and canned foods.* Have children pronounce the names on the various food packages and canned foods.

*   *Use of practical or real-life materials.* Don't forget to use materials like the Yellow Pages, store catalogs, cereal box toy offers, the sports page from the local newspaper, local community center flyers, words for a popular song, and church publications for examples of words illustrating letter–sound relationships.

*   *Always use the new skill in sentences.* Whatever phonic skill children are learning, always ask them to pronounce words that contain the sound and to use the word in a complete sentence.

Reading a Book Together with Your Child

Reading a book with your child should be a pleasurable and meaningful experience. Try to set up a time to read with your child each day. As you read the book, emphasize that reading is interesting and enjoyable. You not only want to enjoy the time reading together with your child but you also want to use a plan that will increase your child's reading abilities. The "proof" of whether or not children are improving in their reading abilities is their ability to actually use new words and new skills in a real story. An analogy can be made to learning to drive a car. While you must learn specific skills, such as looking before changing lanes, entering the highway at a gradual speed, or parallel parking on a city street, and also must pass a written test, the "proof" is not that you can explain how to do it or pass a written test, but it is your ability to perform these acts with a real car on the road (and not get in an accident!). Here are the steps to follow in reading a story with your child:

- Choose a book based on your child's interests.

- Discuss any experiences that your child has had that are related to the story.

- Discuss the pictures in the book, and have your child predict what will happen.

- Take turns with your child reading paragraphs aloud.

- If your child is just learning to read, point to the words as you read them.

- Stop and discuss what is happening in the story at different pages.

- Stop and ask your child the meaning of a word every couple of pages.

- After finishing the story, ask if the predictions were accurate.

- Ask your child if he or she liked the book, and why.

- Together, briefly summarize what the story was about.

- If possible, relate the story to your child's personal experiences.

- For any confusing parts, go back to the story, and reread to clear up misunderstandings.

- Tell your child that it was a wonderful story and how much you enjoyed reading the book together.

Improving Children's Reading Comprehension

As was emphasized earlier, reading is comprehension or understanding. There are many ways to teach children to understand what they are reading. Informally, you can always ask your child to explain what is happening in a story, why the main character of a story acted in a certain way, or to summarize a story you are reading together. The following are additional techniques to use with children in the home to increase their reading comprehension:

- *"Reporter questions"*—who, what, where, when, why, *and* how

  — After reading a page or two of a story or an entire story, ask children a "reporter question" regarding the story, and discuss their answer. For example, ask children: Who is this story about? What is happening? Where did it happen? When is it happening? Why is it happening? How did it happen?

  — After reading a story, make up a sheet with the "reporter questions" across the top, and ask children to write the answers to the "reporter questions" below each question. After children are finished, discuss their responses. Make sure children can give you a complete answer to each question.

- *Finish the story.* Read a story with your child, and stop before you reach the end of the story. Ask your child what he or she thinks will happen in the rest of the story. Discuss your child's responses. Make sure your child understands that more than one word is required to fill in the missing information.

- *What I know.* Provide children with a brief introduction to a story, and show them pictures related to the story. Before reading the story, ask children (or have them write down) what they know about the story and what they would like to know after they finish reading it. After reading the story, ask children what new information they learned and what questions still remain.

- *Branching tree.* After reading a story, ask children to draw a big tree with a trunk and several branches. Together, help children write the story's main idea on the trunk and the important details or main characters on the branches, or write the main idea on the trunk and the sequence of events on the branches.

Increasing Children's Fluency in Reading

The ability to understand ideas in writing is the essence of reading. However, this is only possible if children can first pronounce or decode words with ease—that is, if children can accurately, quickly, and smoothly pronounce and understand written symbols. This ability to pronounce words quickly and smoothly is known as fluency. Here are some ideas to promote fluency at home with children:

- *Read a story or paragraph over and over.* Many times, children do not have the opportunity to read something over and over in school. This repetition helps to develop children's confidence and fluency. Take a favorite book, and ask children to read a page or two aloud, and then ask them to read it again aloud. Discuss with children the benefits of repeating a story or part of a story over and over. If you have a tape recorder, tape your child's first reading, and after repeated readings, tape the same story another time and compare the two tapes.

- *Phrase reading.* Select a story your child is reading, and model reading a paragraph in a word-by-word fashion and in meaningful phrases. Using a pencil (you may want to copy part of the story for ease of marking), divide or slash the sentences into meaningful phrases. Together with your child, read the sentences aloud in meaningful phrases with pauses after each slash. Have your child practice reading this part of the story over and over in meaningful phrases. Discuss with your child the benefits of reading sentences in meaningful phrases, as opposed to word-by-word reading.

- *Use of practical or real-life materials.* Don't forget to use materials like the Yellow Pages, store catalogs, cereal box toy offers, the sports page from the local newspaper, local community center flyers, words for a popular song, and church publications with your child for practicing fluency or reading smoothly.

References

Alexander, P. A., & Jetton, T. L. (2000). Learning from text: A multidimensional and developmental perspective. In M. L. Kamil, P. B. Mosenthal, P. D. Pearson, & R. Barr (Eds.), *Handbook of reading research* (Vol. 3, pp. 285–310). Mahwah, NJ: Lawrence Erlbaum.

Allington, R. L. (1977). If they don't read much, how they ever gonna get good? *Journal of Reading*, 21(1), 57–61.

Allington, R. L. (1983). The reading instruction provided readers of differing abilities. *The Elementary School Journal*, 83(5), 548–559.

Allington, R. L. (2006). *What really matters for struggling readers: Designing research-based programs* (2nd ed.). Boston: Pearson Education.

Allington, R. L., & McGill-Franzen, A. (1989). School response to reading failure: Instruction for Chapter 1 and special education students in grades 2, 4, and 8. *The Elementary School Journal*, 89(5), 529–542.

Allington, R. L., & McGill-Franzen, A. (2003). The impact of summer setback on the reading achievement gap. *Phi Delta Kappan*, 85(1), 68–75.

Allington, R. L., & Walmsley, S. L. (Eds.). (1995). *No quick fix: Rethinking literacy programs in America's elementary schools*. Newark, DE: International Reading Association.

Anderson, R. C. (1994). *The future of reading research*. Technical Report No. 600. Champaign, IL: College of Education, University of Illinois.

Anderson, R. C., Hiebert, E. H., Scott, J. A., & Wilkinson, T. A. (1985). *Becoming a nation of readers: The report of the Commission on Reading*. Champaign, IL: University of Illinois, Center for the Study of Reading.

Apthorp, H. S. (2006). Effects of a supplemental vocabulary program in third-grade reading/language arts. *The Journal of Educational Research*, 100(2), 67–79.

Armbruster, B., Lehr, F., & Osborn, J. (2001). *Put reading first*. Washington, DC: National Institute for Literacy.

Au, K. H. (1993). *Literary instruction in multicultural settings*. Fort Worth, TX: Harcourt Brace Jovanovich.

Ausubel, D. P., & Robinson, F. G. (1969). *School learning: An introduction to educational psychology*. New York: Holt, Rinehart & Winston.

Baumann, J. F., & Duffy, A. M. (1997). *Engaged reading for pleasure and learning: A report from the National Reading Research Center*. Athens, GA: National Reading Research Center.

Blair, Timothy R. (1975). *Relationship of teacher effort and student achievement in reading*. Doctoral dissertation, University of Illinois, 1975.

Blair, Timothy R. (2003). *New teacher's performance-based guide to culturally diverse classrooms*. Boston: Allyn & Bacon.

Brooks, W. (2006). Reading representations of themselves: Urban youth use culture and African American textual features to develop literary understandings. In D. Reinking & D. E. Alvermann (Eds.), *Reading Research Quarterly*, 41, 372–392.

Brown, S. C., & Kysilka, M. L. (2002). *Applying multicultural and global concepts in the classroom and beyond*. Boston: Allyn & Bacon.

Burman, L. E., & Wheaton, L. (2005). *Who gets the child tax credit?* Washington, DC: Tax Policy Center, Urban Institute and Brookings Institution.

Closing the achievement gap (2006). *Quick facts*. Denver, CO: Education Commission of the States.

Coiro, J., Knobel, M., Lankshear, C. & Leu, D. (eds) (2008). *The Handbook of Research on New Literacies*. Mahwah, NJ: Erlbaum.

Combs, A. W. (1982). *A personal approach to teaching: Beliefs that make a difference*. Boston: Allyn & Bacon.

Crawford, P. A., & Zygouris-Coe, V. (2005). All in the family: Connecting home and school with family literacy. *Early Childhood Education Journal*, 33(4), 261–267.

Cunningham, A. E., & Stanovich, K. E. (1998). What reading does for the mind. *American Educator*, 22(1–2), 8–15.

Delpit, L. (1991). A conversation with Lisa Delpit. *Language Arts*, 68(7), 541–547.

Denton, K., & West, J. (2002). *Children's reading and mathematics achievement in kindergarten and first grade*. Washington DC: National Center for Education Statistics.

Diller, D. (1999). Opening the dialogue: Using culture as a tool in teaching your African-American children. *The Reading Teacher*, 52, 820–828.

Dolch, E. W. (1948). *Problems in reading*. Champaign, IL: Garrard Press.

Donahue, P. L., Voelkl, K. E., Campbell, J. R., & Mazzeo, J. (1999, March). *NAEP 1998 reading report card for the nation and states*. Washington, DC: Department of Education.

Durkin, D. (2004). *Teaching them to read* (6th ed.). Boston: Pearson Education.

Edwards, P. A. (2004). *Children's literacy development: Making it happen through school, family, and community involvement*. Boston: Pearson Education.

ESL standards for pre-k–12 students. (1997). Alexandria, VA: Teachers of English of Speakers of Other Languages, Inc.

Flanagan, B. (1997). Beginning teacher finds rewards in urban education. In *info.edu*. University of Illinois at Urbana–Champaign: College of Education.

Garcia, G. E. (1991). Factors influencing the English reading test performance of Spanish-speaking Hispanic students. *Reading Research Quarterly*, 26, 371–392.

Gentile, L. M. (2004). *The oracy instructional guide*. Carlsbad, CA: Dominie Press, Inc.

Gentile, L. M., & McMillan, M. M. (1989). Literacy through literature: Motivating "at risk" students to read and write. Paper presented at the College Reading Association Annual Conference, Philadelphia, PA.

Haberman, M. (1996). The pedagogy of poverty versus good teaching. In W. Ayers & P. Ford (Eds.), *City kids, city teachers: Reports from the front row* (pp. 118–130). New York: The New Press.

Haberman, M. (2005). *Star teachers: The ideology and best practice of effective teachers of diverse children and youth in poverty*. The Haberman Educational Foundation (www.habermanfoundation.org).

Harris, T. L., & Hodges, R. E. (Eds.). (1995). *The literacy dictionary*. Newark, DE: International Reading Association.

Hart, B., & Risley, T. R. (1995). *Meaningful differences in the everyday experience of young American children*. Baltimore, MD: Paul H. Brookes.

Heilman, A. W. (2006). *Phonics in proper perspective* (10th ed.). Upper Saddle River, NJ: Pearson.

Heilman, A. W., Blair, T. R., & Rupley, W. H. (2002). *Principles and practices of teaching reading* (10th ed.). Upper Saddle River, NJ: Merrill-Pearson Education.

Hewson, P., & Kahle, J. B. (2003). Toward equity in science instruction. *WCER Research Highlights*, 15, 2. Madison, WI: Wisconsin Center for Education Research, School of Education, University of Wisconsin.

Hiebert, E. H. (1996). Creating and sustaining a love of literature . . . and the ability to read it. In M. F. Graves, P. van den Broek, & B. M. Taylor (Eds.), *The first R: Every child's right to read* (pp. 15–36). New York: Teachers College Press, and Newark, DE: The International Reading Association.

Hodgkinson, H. L. (1999). Demographic Trends in the U.S. and the State of Florida. Presentation at the University of Central Florida, Orlando, FL, May.

Husbands, K. L., & Shores, J. H. (1950). Measurement of reading for problem solving: A critical review of the literature. *Journal of Educational Research*, 43, 453–65.

International Reading Association. (2009). *IRA position statement on new literacies and 21st century technologies*. Newark, DE: International Reading Association. Retrieved from *http://www.reading.org/General/AboutIRA/Position Statements/21stCenturyLiteracies.aspx*

Johnson, J. P., Livingston, M., Schwartz, R. A., & Slate, J. R. (2000). What makes a good elementary school? A critical examination. *Journal of Educational Research*, 93, 339–348.

Kelley, M., & Clausen-Grace, N. (2006). R5: The sustained silent reading makeover that transformed readers. *The Reading Teacher*, 60, 148–156.

Kozol, J. (1991). *Savage inequalities: Children in America's schools*. New York: The Trumpet Club.

Leu, D. J. & Forzani, E. (2012). New literacies in a Web 2.0, 3.0, 4.0, . . . ∞ world. *Research in the Schools 19*(1). 75–81.

Leu, D.J., Jr., Kinzer, C.K., Coiro, J., & Cammack, D. (2004). Toward a theory of new literacies emerging from the Internet and other information and communication technologies. In R.B. Ruddell & N. Unrau (Eds.), *Theoretical Models and Processes of Reading,* Fifth Edition (1568–1611). International Reading Association: Newark, DE.

Lyon, G. R. (2001). Measuring success: Using assessments and accountability to raise student achievement. Washington, DC: Statement before the Subcommittee on Education Reform, Committee on Education and the Workforce, U.S. House of Representatives, March 8.

Macdonald, J. (1964). An image of man: The learner himself. In R. C. Doll (Ed.), *Individualized instruction*. Washington, DC: Association for Supervision and Curriculum Development, National Education.

Maslow, A. H. (1954). *Motivation and personality*. New York: Harper.

McCarthey, S. J. (2000). Home-school connections: A review of the literature. *The Journal of Educational Research*, 93(3), 145–152.

Moats, L. C. (2001). Overcoming the language gap. *American Educator*, 25(5), 8–9.

Nagy, W., & Herman, P. (1987). Breadth and depth of vocabulary knowledge: Implications for acquisition and instruction. In M. G. McKeown & M. E. Curtis (Eds.), *The nature of vocabulary acquisition* (pp. 19–35). Hillsdale, NJ: Erlbaum.

National Governors Association Center (NCA Center) for Best Practices and Council of Chief State School Officers (CSSO) 2010. *Common Core State Standards for English Language Arts in and Literacy in History/Social Studies, Science and Technical Subjects*. Washington DC: NGA Center and CCSSO.

National Governors Association Center for Best Practices & Council of Chief State School Officers. (2012). *Implementing the Common Core State Standards*. Retrieved from *http://www.corestandards.org/*

National Institute of Child Health and Human Development. (2000). *Report of the National Reading Panel. Teaching children to read: An evidence-based assessment of the scientific research literature on reading and its implications for reading instruction* (NIH Publication No. 00-4769). Washington, DC: U.S. Government Printing Office.

Ogle, D. M. (1986). K-W-L: A teaching model that develops active reading of expository text. *The Reading Teacher,* 39, 564–70.

Palinscar, A. S., & Brown, A. L. (1984). Reciprocal teaching of comprehension-fostering and comprehension-monitoring activities. *Cognition and Instruction,* I, 117–175.

Paris, S. G., Lipson, M. Y., & Wixon, K. G. (1994). Becoming a strategic reader. In R. B. Ruddell, M. R. Ruddell, & H. Singer (Eds.), *Theoretical models and processes of reading* (4th ed.) (pp. 788–810). Newark, DE: International Reading Association.

Partnership for Assessment of Readiness for College and Careers. (2011). *PARCC Model Content Frameworks: English Language Arts/Literacy grades 3–11.* Retrieved from *www.parcconline.org/sites/parcc/files/PARCCMCFELALiteracyAugust2012_FINAL.pdf*

Pearson, P. D. (1997). Transcript from conference *Critical Balances: Early Instruction for Lifelong Reading.* Houston, TX. Reading Online, Posted October 1997, from *http://www.readingonline.org/critical/houston/pearson.htm.*

Pearson, P.D. (2009). The roots of reading comprehension instruction. In S.E. Israel & G.G. Duffy (Eds.), *Handbook of research on reading comprehension.* New York: Routledge, pp.3-31.

Purcell-Gates, V. (1995). *Other people's words: The cycle of low literacy.* Cambridge, MA: Harvard University Press.

Raphael, T. E. (1982). Question-answering strategies for children. *The Reading Teacher*, 39, 516–22.

Rasinski, T., & Padak, N. (2004). Beyond consensus beyond balance: Toward a comprehensive literacy curriculum. *Reading & Writing Quarterly*, 20, 91–102.

Raths, J. (1975a). *Identifying a research problem.* Unpublished paper. Urbana, IL: University of Illinois.

Raths, J. (1975b). Personal communication. Urbana, IL: University of Illinois.

Raths, L. E. (1969). *Teaching for learning.* Columbus, OH: Merrill.

Raths, L. E. (1972). *Meeting the needs of children: Creating trust and security.* Columbus, OH: Merrill.

Raths, L. E., Wassermann, S., Jonas, A., & Rothstein, A. M. (1986). *Teaching for thinking: Theory, strategies, and activities for the classroom.* New York: Teachers College Press, Columbia University.

Rosenshine, B. (2002). Helping students from low-income homes read at grade level. *Journal of Education for Students Placed at Risk*, 7(2), 273–283.

Rosenshine, B., & Meister, C. (1995). Scaffolds for teaching higher-order cognitive strategies. In A. C. Ornstein (Ed.), *Teaching: Theory into practice.* Boston: Allyn & Bacon.

Rosenshine, B., & Stevens, R. (1995). Functions for teaching well-structured tasks. *Journal of Educational Research*, 88, 262–268.

Rowe, M. (1974). Wait-time and rewards as instructional variables, their influence on language logic and fate control: Part 1. Wait-time. *Journal of Research in Science Teaching*, 11, 81–94.

Samuels, S. J. (1988). Decoding and automaticity: Helping poor readers become automatic at word recognition. *The Reading Teacher*, 41, 756–760.

Samuels, S. J. (1997). The method of repeated readings. *The Reading Teacher*, 50, 376–381.

Samuels, S. J. (2002). *Teaching children to read* (2nd ed.). *Video* produced for the National Reading Panel by Widney Communications.

Shanahan, T., Fisher, D., & Frey, N. (2012). The challenge of challenging text. *Educational Leadership*, 69, 58–62.

Sloyer, S. (1982). *Readers theatre: Story dramatization in the classroom.* Urbana, IL: National Council of Teachers of English.

Smith, M. C., & Elish-Piper, L. (2002). Primary-grade educators and adult literacy: Some strategies for assisting low-literate parents. *The Reading Teacher*, 56, 156–165.

Snow, C. E., Burns, M. S., & Griffin, P. (Eds.). (1998). *Preventing reading difficulties in young children.* Washington, DC: National Academy Press.

Taylor, B. M., Pearson, P. D., Clark, K., & Walpole, S. (1999). *Beating the odds in teaching all children to read: Lessons from effective schools and exemplary teachers.* Center for the Improvement of Early Reading Achievement (CIERA) (Rep. No. 2-006). Ann Arbor, MI: University of Michigan School of Education.

Torgesen, J. K., & Hudson, R. F. (2006). Reading fluency: Critical issues for struggling readers. In S. J. Samuels & A. E. Farstrup (Eds.), *What research has to say about fluency instruction.* Newark, DE: International Reading Association.

U.S. Commission on Civil Rights (1992, February). *Civil rights issues facing Asian Americans in the 1990s.* (A report of the United States Commission on Civil Rights.) Washington, DC: author.

Waldbart, A., Meyers, B., & Meyers, J. (2006). Invitations to families in an early literacy support program. *The Reading Teacher*, 59, 774–785.

West, J., Denton, K., & Germino-Hauskin, E. (2000). *America's kindergartners: Findings from the Early Childhood Longitudinal Study, kindergarten class of 1998–1999, Fall 1998.* Washington, DC: U.S. Department of Education, National Center for Education Statistics.

Youth indicators 1996: Trends in the well-being of American youth. (1996). Washington, DC: U.S. Department of Education, National Center for Education Statistics.

Zequeira, C. (2006, June 2). UCF Haitian project aims to erode cultural barriers. *Orlando Sentinel*, 1, p. 7B.

Zygouris-Coe, V. (2006). Personal communication. Orlando, FL: University of Central Florida.

Index

academic engaged time, 10–11
achievement gap, 7–9
activities. *See* teaching activities
adult literacy, 45
African American population, poverty
   statistics of, 6
after-reading strategies, 101–102, 105
Alexander, P.A., 66
Allington, Richard, 7, 10
analytic phonics, 81–82
anchor standards, 110
Anderson, R.C., 62
Apthorp, H.S., 74
Armbruster, Bonnie, 47, 80
Asian population, increase in, 5
assessment
   assessment-instruction, model of,
     28, 29
   continuous, and reflection, 28
   of instructional needs, 25–26
   and priority decision-making, 26–27
   of student needs, 20
Assistive Technology (AT), 117
at-risk students, and critical thinking, 97
Au, K. H., 6
audio books, 117
Ausubel, D. B., 23
automaticity, 40
awareness
   phonemic, 70–72
   phonological, 100
   word, 100

balanced reading instruction, 10, 32
basic service words, 74, 80–81
Baumann, J. F., 44
Becoming a Nation of Readers (Anderson
   et al.), 62
before-reading strategies. *See* prereading
   strategies
behaviors, teacher. *See* teacher behaviors
bilingual resources, 46–48
Blair, Timothy R., 13, 49, 100
blogs, 118
Book Week celebration activity, 125–127
brainstorming, 63, 67
Brooks, W., 5
Brown, A.L., 91
Brown, S. C., 4–5
buddy-reads, 37
Burman, L.E., 6
Burns, M. Susan, 7, 48

Cammack, D., 116
Campbell, J.R., 4
Center for the Study of Reading,
   University of Illinois, 49
Child Becomes a Reader, A, 47
Child Care Aware, 46–47
Children's Book Council, 125, 126
choral speaking, 63
clarifying comprehension task, 106
clarifying questions, 97
Clark, K., 32
classroom wikis, 118
classrooms, current, 4
Clausen-Grace, N., 124
"close" reading, 113
   close reading lesson planning model
     exemplar, 113–114
coaching, 35
Cobb, Amanda, 21–22
Coiro, J., 116
Combs, A. W., 23
Committee on Education and the
   Workforce, 7
Common Core State Standards (CCSS),
   110–114
   anchor standards, 110
   English Language Arts (ELA), 110
   Reading: Foundation Skills, 110
   reading standards in, 110
   teacher behaviors in, 111
   teaching strategies for, 112–113
communication
   with families, 49–52
   of high expectations, 53
comprehension, strategic, 132
comprehension instruction, 12, 16, 90–94,
   132
   parent help with, tips for, 170–171
comprehension tasks, 105–106
consonant activities, 83–84
content-area comprehension, 132
content learning, 16
content reading, and development of
   understanding, 104–107
content words, 74, 132
contextual analysis, 80
continuous assessment, 28
corrective learning, 16
Crawford, P. A., 44
critical comprehension, 12, 90, 132
critical thinking
   and at-risk students, 97
   developing, 96–97

culture
   and background, of students, 21–22,
     44–45
   valuing, 11
cultural diversity. *See* diversity
culturally defined meanings, 23–24
culturally responsive instruction, 6
Cunningham, A.E., 124

Daily Parent, The, 47
decision-making, priority, 26–27
decoding skills, 11, 80, 86
deductive approach, to phonics, 81–82
deletion, phoneme, 71
Delpit, L., 11
Denton, K., 7, 62
dialect, standard and nonstandard, 5
differentiated reading instruction, 10, 32
digital libraries, 118–119
digital texts, 118
Diller, D., 6
direct instruction, 10–11, 133–134
   teaching steps for, 134
diversity, 4–6
   and the achievement gap, 7–9
   benefits of, personal observations,
     16–17
   celebrating, activities for, 39
   within communities, 44–45
   cultural, 5–6
   and effective reading programs,
     9–12
Dolch, Edward, 74
Dole, J.A., 90
Donahue, P.L., 4
Drop Everything And Read (DEAR), 124
Duffy, A. M., 44
Duffy, G.G., 90
Durkin, D., 80
during-reading strategies, 101, 105

early childhood programs, and emergent
   literacy, 14–15
Early Literacy Child-Care Checklist, 47
Educational Resource Information Center
   (ERIC), 46
Edwards, P.A., 11
Elish-Piper, L., 45
emergent literacy stage, 14–15
emotional maturity, of students, 24–25
emotional security, fostering, 24–25
encouragement, providing, 39

engaged time, 32

English as a second language. *See* ESL students

English Language Arts (ELA) standards, 110

environmental print, 7, 63

ERIC Clearinghouse on Elementary and Early Childhood Education, 46

ERIC Clearinghouse on Reading and Communication Skills, 46

ESL Standards for Pre-K–12 Students, 5

ESL students, 5

    myths concerning, 5

    resources for, 46–48

evaluation, of lesson. 36

expectations, communication of, 58–59, 166

experience charts, 64

explicit instruction, 10–11, 133–134

    teaching steps for, 134

expository text, 104

feedback, on student work, 39

Fisher, D., 111

Flanagan, Bonnie, 12

Florida, Literacy and Reading Excellence (FLaRE) project, 48

Florida Online Reading Professional Development (FOR-PD), 48

fluency development, 35, 86–87

    parent help with, tips for, 171

formal reading stage, 15

Forzani, E., 116

Frey, N., 111

frustration instructional level, 25

Garcia, G.E., 74

generative approach, vocabulary development, 76

Gentile, Lance, 64, 97

Germino-Hauskin, E., 62

Glogster, 120

Graded Paragraph Inventory (GPI), 25–26, 135–162

    administration of, 137–141

    examiner's copy, 143–152

    levels in, 136–137

    student's copy, 153–162

    summary form, 142

Griffin, Peg, 7, 48

grouping, of students, 32

groups, instructional, 32

Guide to Early Literacy in Child Care, 46–47

guided reading, 35, 100–102

Guided Reading Plan, 35, 75, 101–102

    for content reading, 104–105, 106

Harris, T. L., 58, 96

Hart, B., 12

Heilman, A. W., 70, 100

"Helping Your Child Go Places through Literacy," 47

Herman, P., 74

Hewson, P., 6

Hiebert, E. H., 7, 9

hierarchy of needs, Maslow, 23

high expectations, communication of, 58–59, 166

high-quality instruction, 9–10, 12

higher-level thinking. *See* critical thinking

Hispanic population

    increase in, 5

    poverty statistics of, 6

Hodges, R. E., 58, 96

Hodgkinson, Harold, 6

Hogan, Ben, 39

home–school connections, strengthening, 50

Hudson, R.F., 86

Husbands, K.L., 104

Illinois Early Learning Project, 48

immigration demographics, 5

INCCIC Online Library, 46

independent instructional level, 25

independent reading, fostering, 124–128

independent reading stage, 15

independent reading/writing activities, 35, 125–128

Indiana University, 46

inductive approach, to phonics, 81–82

inferential comprehension, 90, 132

informal interest survey, 21, 22

informal reading inventories (IRIs), 25–26

    Graded Paragraph Inventory (GPI), 25–26, 135–162. *See also* Graded Paragraph Inventory (GPI)

informing strategy, 90

instruction. *See also specific types of instruction*; teaching strategies

    differentiated, 10, 32

    direct, 10–11, 133–134

    explicit, 10–11, 133–134

    high-quality, 9–10, 12

    scaffolded, 90, 134

instructional learning, 16

instructional levels, 27

    determining, 25–26

instructional needs, students, 25–26

interest survey, informal, 21, 22

International Reading Association (IRA), 116

Internet resources, 46–48

interpretive comprehension, 132

IQ, 13

isolation, phoneme, 71

Jetton, T.L., 66

Jonas, A., 96–97

Just Read, Florida! Initiative, 48

"just-right" instructional level, 25

Kahle, J. B., 6

Kelley, M., 124

Kinzer, C.K., 116

Kidblog, 118

Knobel, M., 116

Kozol, Jonathan, 6

K-W-L strategy, 37, 106

    sample K-W-L chart, 107

Kysilka, M. L., 4–5

language development, and high versus low SES, 11–12

language development, oral, 62–64

language experience approach (LEA), 64

Lankshear, C., 116

Lehr, Fran, 47, 80

lesson planning, 33–40

    and inclusion, 58

letter-sound correspondence, 80

Leu, D.J., Jr., 116

Lipson, M.Y., 104

literacy, adult, 45

literal comprehension, 90, 132

low-income status. *See* poverty

Lyon, G. R., 7

Macdonald, James, 23

Maslow, Abraham, 23

math skills and strategies, 106

Mazzeo, J., 4

maturity, emotional, of students, 24–25

McCarthey, S. J., 44–45

McGill-Franzen, A., 10

McMillan, M. M., 97

meaning, types of, 23–24

meaning words, 74, 132

Meister, C., 90

metacognition, 90, 104, 132

Meyers, B., 44

Meyers, J., 44

minority students. *See* diversity

Moats, L.C., 74

modeling strategy, 90

Nagy, W., 74

National Association of Child Care Resource and Referral Agencies (NACCRRA), 47

National Center for Education Statistics (NCES), 7
National Center for Family Literacy, 46
National Child Care Information Center (NCCIC), 46–47
National Governors Association Center for Best Practices & Council of Chief State School Officers, 110
National Institute for Literacy (NIFL), 46, 47
National Institute of Child Health and Human Development (NICHD), 46, 47
National Parent Information Network (NPIN), 46
National Reading Panel, 14, 47, 48
National Reading Research Center (NRRC), 44
needs
    hierarchy of, Maslow, 23
    personal, of students, 22–24
non-English speakers. See ESL students

Ogle, D., 106
onsets, 82
on-task behavior. See academic engaged time
opportunity to learn, 6–7, 10–11, 32
optimistic criteria/causes, 13
Oracy Instructional Guide (Gentile), 64
oral language development, 62–64
Osborn, Jean, 47, 80

Padak, N., 86
paired readings, 87
pair-share, 112
Palinscar, A.S., 91
parent guide for helping children read, 163–171
    high expectations, communicating, 166
    specific techniques for improving reading skills, 166–171
    ten tips for, 164–165
parents and children's reading ability, 14–15
    expectations of, 52
    guide for helping children read. See parent guide for helping children read
    help for, 46–49
    influence of on children, 44
    involving, 44–45, 49–52
    literacy of, 45
    personal observations of, 52–54
    and poverty effects, 7–9
    resources for, 46–49
Paris, S.G., 104

Partnership for Assessment of Readiness for College and Careers, 111
Partnership for Reading, 46, 47
Pearson, P. D., 9, 32, 90
personal meanings, 23–24
phonemes, 70
    blending words, 71
    phoneme deletion, 71
    phoneme isolation, 71
    phoneme segmentation, 71
    phoneme substitution, 71
phonemic awareness, 70–72
phonics instruction, 80–84
    and parent help, techniques for, 168–169
    analytic phonics, 81–82
phonograms, 82
phonological awareness, 100
phrase reading, 86–87, 171
poverty, 6–9
    demographics of, 6
    and reading, 9
    and student achievement, 7–9
    and vocabulary development, 74
practice, importance of, 40, 76
predicting comprehension task, 105
prefix activities, 84
pre-planning, 33–34
prereading strategies, 90, 91, 101, 104–105
prerequisite knowledge, 66
Preventing Reading Difficulties in Young Children, 48
print awareness, 100
print environment, 7, 63
prior knowledge, developing, 66–67
priority decision-making, 26–27
probing questions, 97
professional development, of teachers, 21–22
public schools
    current classroom climate, 4
    and inequality, 6
Purcell-Gates, V., 44
Put Reading First: Helping Your Child Learn to Read, 46, 47

Question-Answer Relationships (QAR) strategy, 92
questions
    clarifying, 97
    developing and answering, comprehension task, 105

R5 strategy, 124
Raphael, T.E., 92
Rasinski, T., 86

Raths, James, 13, 20, 24–25
Raths, Louis, 24, 96–97
read alouds, 35
readers' theater, 87
readiness, review, and motivation, as instructional components, 34
reading
    importance of, 9
    instruction. See reading instruction
    paired, 87
    phrase, 86–87, 171
    programs, effective, and diversity, 9–12
    recreational, promoting, 127–128
    repeated, 86
    shared, 100–101
    skills and strategies, capsule review of, 129–132
    together, parent and child, tips for, 169–170
reading comprehension. See comprehension instruction
reading development, stages of, 14
    emergent literacy, 14–15
    formal reading, 15
    independent reading, 15
    wide reading, 15
reading fluency. See fluency development
reading instruction
    balanced, 10, 32
    differentiated, 10, 32
    increasing student ability, specific techniques for, 166–171
    instructional components, essential, 34–36
    overview of, 14–16
    and practice, necessity of, 40
    pre-planning considerations, 33–34
    reading development, stages of, 14–15
    reading process, 10, 14
    reading program, complete, 15–16
    and teacher behavior, 36–39
    teaching reading, 33–40
"reading" students, 20–21
Reading Tips for Parents, 47
reciprocal teaching, 105–106
recreational learning, 16
recreational reading/writing, promoting, 127–128
reflection
    and continuous assessment, 28
    and evaluation, of reading plan, 36
repeated reading, 86
"reporter questions" strategy, 92, 170
resources, for teachers and parents, 46–49

retelling technique, 35
rhyming words, 72
rimes, 82
Risley, T. R., 12
Robinson, F. G., 23
Roehler, L.R., 90
Rosenshine, B., 4, 33, 90
Rothstein, A.M., 96–97
Rowe, M., 91
Rupley, W.H., 100

Samuels, S. J., 14, 80, 86
*Savage Inequalities: Children in
   America's Schools* (Kozol), 6
scaffolded instruction, 90, 134
school–home connections, strengthening, 50
science skills and strategies, 106
screen readers, 117
second-language learning. *See* ESL
   students
segmentation, phoneme, 71
self-perceptions, of students, 22–24
semantic maps, 67, 76
semantics, 80
service words, basic, 74, 80–81
Sesame Street, 15
Shanahan, T., 111
shared reading, 100–101
sight-word approach, 80–81
sight words, 74, 80–81
   and parent help, techniques for, 167
single mothers, and poverty, 6
skill/strategy development, 35
Shores, J. H., 104
Sloyer, S., 87
Smith, M. C., 45
Snow, Katherine, 7, 48
social studies strategies, 106
socioeconomic status (SES). *See also*
   poverty
      low versus high, and language
         development, 11–12
software for reading program, 118, 119,
   120
SouthEast Initiatives Regional Technology
   in Education Consortium (SEIR*TEC),
   48
Spanish-language resources, 46–48
speech synthesizers, 118
Standard English, 5
Stanovich, K.E., 124
Starting Out Right, 48
Stevens, R., 33
story retelling, 35
strategic comprehension, 132
strategies. *See* teaching strategies
structural analysis, 80, 82

students
   achievement of, and teacher quality,
      13
   at-risk, and critical thinking, 97
   background experiences and culture
      of, 21–22
   emotional maturity of, 24–25
   encouragement and rewarding of, 39
   and feedback, providing, 39
   grouping of, 32
   instructional levels of, determining,
      25–26
   instructional needs of, 25–26
   needs of, assessing, 20
   needs of, unmet, effects of, 28
   performance of, factors affecting,
      7–9
   personal observations of, 41
   "reading" of, 20–21
   self-perceptions and needs of, 22–24
   strengths of, focusing on, 11
   success in a global economy and
      society, 110
Subcommittee on Education Reform, 7
substitution, phoneme, 71
suffix activities, 84
summarizing comprehension task, 106
Sustained Silent Reading (SSR), 124
syllable activities, 84

Tax Policy Center, 6
Taylor, B.M., 32
teacher behaviors
   in Common Core State Standards
      (CCSS) based reading instruction,
      111
   in communicating high expectations,
      58
   in comprehension development, 91
   in content reading, and development
      of understanding, 104
   in critical thinking development, 96
   in fluency development, 86
   in guided reading, 100
   in independent reading development,
      124–125
   in oral language development, 62
   in phonemic awareness development,
      70
   in phonics and word recognition
      instruction, 81
   in prior knowledge development, 66
   in reading instruction, effective,
      36–39
   in using technology in the reading
      program, 117
   in vocabulary development, 74–75

teachers. *See also* teacher behaviors;
   teaching activities; teaching strategies
      behaviors of, in reading instruction,
         effective, 36–39, 58
      effort of, 13–14
      and high expectations,
         communicating, 58–59
      and high-quality instruction,
         responsibility for, 12
      and parents, resources for, 46–49
      personal observations of, 16–17, 28
      professional development of, 21–22
      quality of, and student achievement, 13
      and self-monitoring, 33
      and student emotional security,
         fostering, 24–25
      student feelings toward, personal
         observations, 41
      and student unmet needs, effect of, 28
teaching activities
   Assistive Technology (AT) tools, 117
   in comprehension development,
      92–94
   in phonemic awareness development,
      71–72
   for phonics and word recognition
      instruction, 82–84
   for using technology in the reading
      program, 117–121
   in vocabulary development, 76–77
Teaching for Thinking (Raths et al.),
   96–97
teaching strategies
   for Common Core State Standards
      (CCSS) based reading instruction,
      112–113
   for communication of high
      expectations, 58–59
   for comprehension development,
      91–92
   for content reading, and development
      of understanding, 104–107
   in critical thinking development,
      96–97
   for fluency development, 86–87
   for guided reading, 100–102
   for independent reading development,
      125–128
   for oral language development, 63–64
   for phonemic awareness instruction,
      70–71
   for phonics and word recognition
      instruction, 81–82
   for prior knowledge development,
      66–67
   for vocabulary development, 75–76

technology for the reading program,
116–121
    Assistive Technology (AT) tools, 117
    blogs, 118
    classroom wikis, 118
    digital texts, 118–119
    digital libraries, 118–119
    digital storytelling, writing, and
       presentation applications, 119
    information and communication
       technologies (ICTs), 116
    software for outlining, mapping, 120
    tablets and mobile applications, 120
    teacher behaviors needed, 117
    teaching tools and activities,
       117–121
    and Twitter, 120–121
    websites for storytelling projects,
       119–120
    and Wordle, 121
television viewing, children and, 165
thinking activities, 35
"think-time," 91–92
time-on-task. *See* academic engaged time
Torgesen, J.K., 86
transfer, 40
translation, of school messages, 52
Twitter, 120–121

University of Central Florida, 21, 48
University of Illinois at Urbana–
    Champaign, 46
U.S. Census Bureau, 21
U.S. Commission on Civil Rights, 45
U.S. Department of Education, 46, 47
    English- and Spanish-language
       resources of, 46–48

vocabulary development, 35, 74–77, 132
Voelkl, K.E., 4
visual aids, 66–67
vowel activities, 83–84

"wait-time," 91–92
Walmsley, S. L.,10
Waldbart, A., 44
Walpole, S., 32
Wassermann, S., 96–97
websites, 118–121
    for animation/avatars, 119
    for creating a video/movie, 119
    for digital libraries, 119
    for evaluating educational
       applications, 120
    Glogster, 120
    Kidblog, 118
    Twitter, 120–121
    for writing/storyboards, 119–120

West, J., 7, 62
Wheaton, L., 6
whole-word approach, vocabulary
    development, 75, 81
wide-reading stage, 15
Wixon, K.G., 104
word awareness, 100
"word clouds," 121
word families, 82
word identification skills and strategies,
    11, 16, 130–131
"word poverty," 74
word recognition instruction, 80–84
words
    awareness, word, 100
    basic service, 74, 80–81
    blending of, 71
    content, 74, 132
    families, word, 82
    meaning, 74, 132
    sight, 74, 80–81, 167
    whole-word approach to, 75, 81
writing, recreational, promoting, 127–128

Zequeria, C., 21
Zygouris-Coe, V., 44, 48-50